There are a number of organizing books out there with helpful organizing tips. Very few are written to educate the public about the options of getting help. This is one of the few. This road map takes you from acknowledging the need for help to shining a light on the many paths to success. As a veteran Certified Professional Organizer, I highly recommend I'm Right Here, 10 Ways to Get Help with Hoarding and Chronic Disorganization *to potential clients and colleagues.*

– **Standolyn Robertson, CPO®** – Organizing Expert for the Emmy nominated show Hoarders on A&E Network and Author of *Managing Client Expectations for Organizing Professionals*

'I'm Right Here serves up insightful advice with a big portion of hope. This is a must-read if you're searching for the best way to get help with chronic disorganization and hoarding behavior challenges. Jill thoughtfully shares her experiences as a Professional Organizer, along with interviews of industry experts who compassionately and non-judgmentally

describe their perspectives and approaches for helping clients. Included are numerous resources such as classes, publications, and websites. For you, professionals, family members, or friends of folks challenged by chronic disorganization or hoarding behavior. This easy-to-read book is *your essential go-to guide."*

– **Linda Samuels, CPO-CD®, CVPO™**,
Professional Organizer & Author of
The Other Side of Organized

I'm Right Here, *the book's title, gives you the idea, that whenever you are ready to work on organizing your things, thoughts or time, these professionals are here. The first call takes courage, and it's also a signal that you're pretty well ready to start. Not perfectly ready, but ready enough. We are guides. We are educators, We are listeners. We hold the future vision and the hope until you can see it for yourself. We often believe in our client's capabilities more then they do at first. And then they grow. Many see a therapist for the emotional issues and see one of us alongside for the practical; both perspectives assist you in moving forward, creating the peace you desire, and achieving your potential.*

– **Sue West, CPO-CD®, MA**,
Clinical Mental Health Counseling,
ICD® Master Trainer

As I read this book, I could hear Jill's calm voice talking to me. I have known Jill for years. She has this wonderful way of making any situation, no matter how challenging, feel OK. Jill presents that same feeling here in this book. A feeling that, no matter how challenging the home or the problem with clutter, it will be OK. The explanations of the different organizing approaches are great. Unless you are a professional organizer, I bet you didn't know that there are so many different approaches available for organizing assistance. This book is also an essential reference tool for social workers and therapists. They, too, need to know about the variety of organizing approaches available to their clients.

– **Diane N. Quintana, CPO-CD®, CPO®**,
Professional Organizer and Co-Author of
Filled Up and Overflowing: What to do When Life Events, Chronic Disorganization, or Hoarding Go Overboard

This fascinating book describes how professional organizers help people who are burdened by their life-long issues with disorganization. Different methodologies are examined and how they unfold over the course of time when a professional organizer is working with a client. This examination provides the reader with a clear idea of how professional organizers work. Moreover, Jill uncovers the soul of the work: the relationship between the professional organizer and the client. Jill shines a light on the organizers' compassion for their clients, the deep trust the clients have in their organizers, and hope they both have in the work they are doing together to create a better life for the client.

– **Denise B. Lee, CPO®, CSA**,
Professional Organizer and Organizer Coach

I'M RIGHT HERE

I'M RIGHT HERE

10 Ways to Get Help for Hoarding
and Chronic Disorganization

JILL B. YESKO

ACADEMY
PRESS

Copyright © 2021 Discover Organizing Inc. All rights reserved.

No part of this publication shall be reproduced, transmitted, or sold in whole or in part in any form without prior written consent of the author, except as provided by the United States of America copyright law. Any unauthorized usage of the text without express written permission of the publisher is a violation of the author's copyright and is illegal and punishable by law. All trademarks and registered trademarks appearing in this guide are the property of their respective owners.

For permission requests, write to the below address:

Jill B. Yesko
Discover Organizing Inc.
98 Vanadium Road, Building D
Bridgeville, PA 15017

The opinions expressed by the Author are not necessarily those held by PYP Academy Press.

Ordering Information: Quantity sales and special discounts are available on quantity purchases by corporations, associations, and others. For details, contact the author at jill@discoverorganizing.com.

Edited by: Tamera Bryant, Andrea Glass, August Li
Cover design by: Cornelia Murariu
Original bench design by: Nathan C. Yesko
Typeset by: Medlar Publishing Solutions Pvt Ltd., India
Photo credit: Katie Morris

Printed in the United States of America.

ISBN: 978-1-951591-70-0 (paperback)
ISBN: 978-1-951591-71-7 (hardcover)
ISBN: 978-1-951591-72-4 (ebook)

Library of Congress Control Number: 2021908146

First edition, May, 2021

The information contained within this book is strictly for informational purposes. The material may include information, products, or services by third parties. As such, the Author and Publisher do not assume responsibility or liability for any third-party material or opinions. The publisher is not responsible for websites (or their content) that are not owned by the publisher. Readers are advised to do their own due diligence when it comes to making decisions.

The mission of the Publish Your Purpose Academy Press is to discover and publish authors who are striving to make a difference in the world. We give underrepresented voices power and a stage to share their stories, speak their truth, and impact their communities. Do you have a book idea you would like us to consider publishing? Please visit PublishYourPurposePress.com for more information.

PYP Academy Press
141 Weston Street, #155
Hartford, CT, 06141

To my children, Nathan and Mary, who taught me everything.

*"…anything human is mentionable and anything mentionable is manageable.
The mentioning can be difficult too, but both can be done if we're surrounded by love and trust."*
Fred Rogers

CONTENTS

Foreword by Judith Kolberg . . . . *xv*
Introduction . . . . *xix*
My Story . . . . *xxvii*
Assess Yourself: The ICD® Clutter Quality of Life Scale™ . *xxxv*
About the Methods . . . . *xxxvii*

Method 1:   Hands-On Organizing One-on-One with a Professional Organizer 1

Method 2:   Hands-on Organizing with a Professional Organizing Team 17

Method 3:   Brain-Based Specialty Organizing and Coaching 23

Method 4:   Virtual Professional Organizing and Coaching 33

Method 5: Hybrid Organizing Services:
Collaboration between Professional
Organizers and Coaches 39

Method 6: Organizing Classes 43

Method 7: Clutter Support Groups 51

Method 8: Books and Research Publications. 55

Method 9: Online Resources 59

Method 10: Television Shows 67

Afterword. *79*
Appendix *81*
Acknowledgments. *91*
About the Author *93*
Hire Jill to Speak *95*
About Discover Organizing. *97*

FOREWORD

by Judith Kolberg

Nobody really knows how organization skills evolved. But sorting, categorizing, containing stuff, and keeping things handy and accessible, the things we think of when we use the term *organization*, have always seemed to serve humanity well. You might think that after this long history, whatever must be said about organization and disorganization has been said. Not so. In *I'm Right Here: 10 Ways to Get Help for Hoarding and Chronic Disorganization*, Jill Yesko reiterates the organization principles and practices worth repeating. But here's the thoughtful, compelling idea she brings to the old organizing table: there are ten ways to get organized! We're not talking technique here, though that's mentioned too. We're talking actual delivery methods: ten different ways you, as a person in need of organizing, can have the knowledge and systems imparted to you.

For many people, this is what has been missing in their quest to get organized: not what the techniques are per se, but what the ways are! For this, Yesko has turned to experts, professionals who have honed their expertise AND the way they deliver that expertise. Well-written and simply defined, this book allows a reader to consider a choice of how they want the improvement of their organizing skills to happen. Live? Virtual? One-on-one or with a team? Maybe a class or a support group? Perhaps book learning is best, or an online experience? Or a combination of ways? And the expert is *right there*. They are experienced and compassionate, requirements for helping anyone get organized.

This book is great for professional organizers and productivity consultants who need a more well-rounded way to reach their clients. It's practical for allies in the disorganization trade, like psychologists. And, for those struggling with chronic disorganization or hoarding behaviors, it's a must read. I've added it to my reference bookshelf!

About Judith Kolberg

Judith Kolberg is credited with launching an entire field of professional organizing specifically dedicated to addressing the needs of individuals who are challenged by chronic disorganization (CD). In 1989, Kolberg founded FileHeads, a professional organizing company, and she's been a member of the National Association of Productivity & Organizing Professionals (NAPO) since 1990. In the early 1990s, Judith noticed that certain clients didn't respond well to traditional organizing techniques. She developed the term *chronic disorganization* to describe this group and founded the National Study Group on Chronic Disorganization, which would later become the Institute for Challenging Disorganization® (ICD).

Her innovative methods have made organizing breakthroughs for adults with ADHD, chronic disorganization, and hoarding. A recipient of NAPO's prestigious Founders' Award in 1996, Kolberg has authored numerous special reports on organizing and six books, including *Conquering Chronic Disorganization* and *ADD-Friendly Ways to Organize Your Life*, co-authored with Kathleen Nadeau, Ph.D. Select books are recommended reading by the Board of Certification for Professional Organizers or required by various ICD Certification/Certificate programs. In all, her books have sold a quarter of a million copies in the US, England, Korea, The Netherlands, China, France, Mexico, and Japan.

INTRODUCTION

What does it really mean to be disorganized? Do we think of messy homes, scattered piles of paper, and lost keys? Maybe we think of people who don't meet us for lunch on time or who are late for…everything, a lot. We could also think of being disorganized as being unprepared, or as having too much stuff for the space in which we live.

There are different levels of disorganization, at least from the point of view of a professional organizer (PO). We work with clients every day who are experiencing situational as well as chronic disorganization. Situational disorganization presents itself when there's a major life circumstance, such as a new baby, a divorce, a career change, or a death in the family. Up until that identifiable point in time, all has seemed under control. We listen for cues from our clients such as "before the baby came, I was so organized," or "the house was always in order, but when my husband lost his job and was home, it was like I forgot how to do everything that kept the house running smoothly."

Sometimes the successful daily structures that keep life more predictable and less chaotic need only a slight disruption (not all changes are catastrophic) to alter a lifestyle that had been "working." When particular items pile up or specific rooms experience overflow, but not the whole house, it can be an indicator that something is not systemically working in those spaces. After some organizing intervention, the implementation of new workflows, and the client's commitment to keep those new practices in motion, the fix can and usually does become sustainable.

What is Chronic Disorganization?

To some people, the term *chronic disorganization* sounds ominous, like an incurable, terminal disease. Other people react by rolling their eyes or, with raised eyebrows, imply that it's a made-up condition, one yet to be proven a legitimate problem. In my career as a PO, it's been difficult to not only explain exactly what I do, but also to adequately and convincingly explain chronic disorganization (CD). Understanding CD takes time, empathy, and the ability to dive deeply into a topic that has driven many of those who suffer (and those who live with them) to despair and hopelessness.

The Institute for Challenging Disorganization defines chronic disorganization (CD) as "disorganization that persists over a long period of time, frequently undermines quality of life, and recurs despite repeated self-help attempts. Chronic disorganization may be present with brain-based challenges such as ADHD, anxiety, depression, hoarding disorder, post-traumatic stress disorder, and traumatic brain injury."

The Institute for Challenging Disorganization, an educational nonprofit organization, began as The National Study Group on Chronic Disorganization in 1992. Its mission is to provide education, research, and strategies to benefit people affected by CD and the professionals who work with them. In my professional practice, I've witnessed CD in many forms and have found it to be one of the most misunderstood conditions among my clientele.

What About Hoarding?

The Merriam Webster Dictionary defines hoarding as "the compulsion to continuously accumulate a variety of items that are often considered useless or worthless to others, accompanied by an inability to discard the items without great distress". Let's break that down. The key words and phrases here are *compulsion, continually accumulate*, and *inability to discard*. Hoarding behaviors have long been associated with obsessive-compulsive disorder, or OCD. While OCD can coexist with hoarding disorder, it isn't necessarily evident or prevalent in an individual who's hoarding.

Hoarding is part of a person's behavior, but it doesn't define who a person is, which is why you won't read the term *hoarder* in my book unless it's part of the title of the popular television series. Labeling someone a hoarder is harmful and brings judgment and shame into the organizing atmosphere.

Who Can Benefit from this Book?

As I began writing this book, I realized I was going to reach a wider audience than I originally intended. I first and foremost wanted readers who are suffering from CD (of any kind) to understand a little more about the people who've devoted their professional lives to helping those who suffer navigate the painful path this condition and its consequences have on their daily lives. I was, and continue to be, inspired by the professionals who have done the hands-on labor of helping people sort through and make decisions about their possessions, in less than comfortable environments, with clients who don't always want their help but need it. I interviewed ten of my colleagues who, like me, have worked in situations that are not ideal, with clients who inch along toward success instead of bounding toward the finish line.

This book serves as an educational tool for those who have one or more aspects of CD. It also may help those who are dealing with one or more brain-based challenges avoid self-misdiagnoses. For example, a person who believes they have hoarding disorder may actually be accumulating items due to ADHD or clinical depression. It's my hope that they will share their individual symptoms and daily challenges with a medical or mental health professional who can correctly diagnose and treat them with care.

As the writing evolved, I realized that this book could assist social workers, physicians, psychologists, and those in the nursing profession who may be the first person (and possibly the last in a discharge situation) to meet with those in crisis. I've found that many of those suffering from CD usually stay hidden in their environment until there's a true medical (this includes mental health) emergency that forces them to seek care and treatment. If those helping professionals have more understanding of this condition and its effects on those suffering, they may be better prepared to offer the right guidance and to share available and appropriate resources.

Social workers and case managers in hospitals and community health centers usually make referrals based on the prioritized needs of their clients. There are times when comorbidity issues are placed lower in importance, but they shouldn't be neglected altogether. I'm hoping this book will help mental health clinicians see how qualified POs can participate in the success of their clients through collaborative therapy.

If this book closes the gap between those who are suffering and those who can help them, then it will be a success. Accessible, nonjudgmental, expert help is an important objective of this book and is within reach of those who need it. Whether the help is online, in person in the home, at a weekly support group, in a book, a podcast, or over the phone, it's there.

In order to provide more insight into the people behind the profession and to ease any concerns that professional organizers are judgmental or critical of their client's behaviors, backgrounds, or environments, I have chosen to feature the work of ten of my colleagues. I have observed each of their careers in organizing for years and feel that they exemplify and portray empathy, dedication, unique approaches, and compelling perspectives in their practices. The professionals featured in this book have built their businesses with the same common denominators: compassion, kindness, patience, and understanding for each of their clients. All of these women have furthered their own study to understand and work with clients presenting with chronic disorganization. They are aptly suited and fully prepared to help clients who face major challenges to daily organization such as ADHD, OCD, hoarding disorder, depression, and anxiety.

It is vital to have experience and education to work with clients with hoarding disorder and chronic disorganization. The Institute for Challenging Disorganization® (ICD) has provided each of our featured professional organizers with various education levels. Their applied skills are evident in their years of positive experiences with their clients. Please see the Appendix for a more detailed explanation of their impressive credentials and achievements.

Featured Professional Organizers in this book

Linda Samuels, CPO-CD®, CVPO™
Janine Adams, CPO®
Sue West, CPO-CD, MA, Clinical Mental Health Counseling, ICD® Master Trainer

Introduction

Alice Price, CPO-CD, COC®
Cris Sgrott, CPO®, CPO-CD, SMM-C®, ICD Master Trainer
Denise Lee, CPO, CSA®
Sheila Delson, CPO-CD
Vickie Dellaquila, CPO, CPO-CD, ICD Master Trainer
Diane Quintana, CPO, CPO-CD, ICD Master Trainer
Jonda Beattie, M.Ed.

Credential Acronym Definitions

CPO-CD	Certified Professional Organizer in Chronic Disorganization
CPO	Certified Professional Organizer
CSA	Certified Senior Advisor
CVPO	Certified Virtual Professional Organizer
M.A.	Master of Arts
M.Ed.	Master of Science in Education

MY STORY

Professional organizers experienced growth in their business as a result of the media exposure by reality TV shows like *Hoarders* (A&E) and *Hoarding: Buried Alive* (TLC). Books on the topic were published and devoured. Julie Morgenstern's *Organizing from the Inside Out* focused on the reasons people become disorganized and offered step-by-step solutions. The book was a best seller and got Oprah Winfrey's attention. Another celebrity PO and friend of Oprah was straight-talking Peter Walsh, who wrote *It's Just Too Much*. Both books became primers in my own company, and I still use them as a part of the company's orientation program for new team members.

I joined the National Association of Productivity & Organizing Professionals (NAPO) in 2004, one year after starting my own organizing business. Before that, I had been working long hours as director of human resources in a psychiatric hospital for children and was seeking something that would allow me to be more present for my children. The answer came in the spring of 2003. Driving along Banksville Road in Pittsburgh, on my way home from a meeting downtown, I spotted a billboard with the message: "Say Bye-Bye to Clutter! Call me today!" The larger-than-life face of a confident-looking woman was smiling down at me. It was a beacon! It was a literal sign!

The next day I called the beaming woman, Patty Kreamer, and asked if she was hiring. Politely, she said, "No, I don't have employees" and encouraged me to start my own business. She suggested that I check out NAPO's website (www.NAPO.net) and invited me to join her Pittsburgh group of POs when I was up and running.

So at the age of thirty-four, I formed a sole proprietorship with the ever-so-catchy and affirming name of "You Are Organized!" I advertised at the local mailbox and copy center. The phone began to ring, and thankfully, it hasn't stopped since. I don't mean to oversimplify or to make it sound like starting a business while working full time and raising two kids as a divorced mom was easy. It wasn't. Leaving my career and regular salary (and benefits) behind was a huge financial risk. I was still working my regular schedule of forty hours at the hospital then, and I worked nights and weekends here and there to build my clientele. After six months of paying babysitters and missing a few soccer games, I was able to go out on my own. Because there was no established career path for my new field of work, my qualifications were basically a combined professional career of social work and human resources. Luckily, I knew enough to

My Story

get started, and the skills acquired from those careers prepared me well to find and connect my new clients to the services they needed and to later hire several employees in my own firm, Discover Organizing Inc., which I formed as an S-corporation in 2005.

I truly enjoyed my work as a professional organizer from the very beginning, and I felt like I was really good at helping people. I didn't judge my clients one iota for having three of the same toaster ovens or owning hundreds of Precious Moments figurines. If they had overstuffed closets, garages, attics, and basements, I was there to help them sort it, organize it, and discard it if they wanted to let it go. If they didn't want to let go, we talked about it, and if we needed to talk about it some more, we did. The overly cluttered home became my specialty. I organized hundreds of kitchens, made over bedroom closets, installed multiple types of shelving and garage systems, and implemented beautiful and gleaming organizing supplies in people's homes, offices, RVs, and warehouses. I could look at a space and just KNOW whether an item would fit, how many bins would line up on a shelf, and when a client's floor and space plan would succeed—and when it would fail.

I had a basic understanding of best practices but no idea of what hoarding behaviors or CD traits were. My first big challenge came when I couldn't make a dent in one client's basement. I couldn't clear even one square foot of space! I would arrive cheerfully each week with a new strategy for sorting and deciding, for shredding and recycling. Each week, hardly anything moved out. The rest of the house was filled with paper piles. The client was frustrated, but surprisingly, not with me! Still, I felt ineffectual, worthless to her. I offered to stop coming. She said that even though she was struggling, she trusted me (this was huge) and was learning a lot from me. She told me that she mentally rehearsed the practices, phrases, and behaviors I modeled to stop more paper from coming in, even when I wasn't there. She had hired me to help her deal with letting go of the piles of information, memories, and unopened mail she had let accumulate for decades. In the process, she was learning more about herself. It was an incredible feeling for me to see her awareness grow with each session. Her paper piles, diminishing each week, were an albatross she no longer needed. More importantly, they were something she no longer *wanted*.

The very type of client I had been afraid of, the one whose space I couldn't transform, was the very client I began to attract, adhere to, and work with as my business grew. The chronically disorganized client became someone I couldn't wait to work with, hated to leave, and thought about while I was walking my dogs, standing in line at the grocery store, and making dinner.

I read every book I could get my hands on to help each client create a unique and successful strategy. I went to every NAPO and Institute for Challenging Disorganization (ICD) conference I could afford and attended teleclasses as often as possible. I recalled my social work days, where I worked with clients by using their strengths to find creative ways to help them climb over incredibly high walls of doubt, anger, and shame. My heart beat faster when I walked into a home that had good intentions and unrealized dreams. The hobbies strewn all over the creative client's second bedroom, kitchen, and dining room told me how much she loved to make things and sew new creations. The cluttered kitchen of the busy mother told me how much more time she spent playing with her children and reading to them than scrubbing the pots and pans. The tools spread across the garage of the retired veteran told me how much he loved helping his neighbors and family repair their homes and cars while he neglected to take care of his own home.

I was raised in a household where neatness not only counted, it was required. We were to have nothing on our floors except furniture. At some point in my childhood, I remember developing a small fear that I had left something less than perfect in my bedroom while I was at school or at a sleepover. I knew my mother would periodically and quite randomly inspect our rooms for any signs of clutter when I was absent from the house. The consequences for having items not put away properly were *not* desirable. If we left something out, like an errant sock on the floor because we missed the hamper, or a pair of shoes slipped off after school but not put in the shoe chest, our random worldly goods were scooped up and placed in a holding area for return—but only if we earned them back.

Chores (and extra chores) were available at all times. We had a color-coded chore chart that Mom lovingly laminated and rotated so we wouldn't get bored doing the same chore repeatedly. The chores assigned to us for not putting things back where they belonged were the chores we avoided at all costs. Mom was strict, she was orderly, and she was organized.

Our house actually had a routine preventative maintenance program. Bills were always paid on time, and Mom habitually saved portions of her paychecks for her retirement. My father was also neat and tidy. He kept prioritized daily task lists, which he created every morning and tucked neatly in his shirt pocket. He groomed the yard meticulously, grew and trimmed beautiful rose bushes, and took excellent care of the sports cars he loved.

My mother grew up in a large house with her parents, one older brother, and fourteen younger siblings. That's right, sixteen children. That's a LOT of laundry, meals, cleanup, and other stuff. I'm sure that heavily monitored and maintained schedules and rules about clutter were what kept my grandparents sane. Also, they had housekeepers. So, you see, *I get it*. I understand the need for so much structure, even for our small nuclear family of four.

When it was time for me to run my own household, I knew on some inherent level that this level of order wasn't something I could ask of my own children or maintain with my own lifestyle. I created age-appropriate routines that my children could follow, and they did. I allowed them to keep their rooms how they wanted, within reason, and they did a really good job, with the biggest periods of chaos being their teen years. I believe we had balance, not perfection. Our home was clean, but there were nights when a stray drinking glass was left on the counter, piles of mail sat on the dining room table, and even little pink socks, left behind by a tired little girl tottering off to bed, dotted the stairs. I allowed my refrigerator to be covered with works of art from my son and carefully drawn renditions of me (with crazy hair and very long fingers and feet) from my small daughter. I needed a *little* chaos, and I wanted to not worry about cleaning up after everything we did. I knew that as Type A as I am, I could never attain the level of perfection that celebrity role models like Martha Stewart defined (or that my own mother would want).

I craved the kind of home that my family could relax in but that was still tidy and organized. I came to believe that most of my clients wanted this too. I became a partner to them in their own personal journey to achieve the type of home they always wanted. A successful home environment looks different for everyone. The biggest lesson I learned was that I could gently stretch my clients to see how their new systems could give them peace of mind and also make sure they knew it was always up to them to make it happen. I was only a guide.

ASSESS YOURSELF: THE ICD® CLUTTER QUALITY OF LIFE SCALE™

The Clutter Quality of Life Scale (CQLS) was developed by Catherine Roster of the University of New Mexico in collaboration with ICD. It measures four main impacts of clutter in someone's life: emotional, social, livability of space, and financial, with a higher score denoting a higher level of impact. Answers to questions such as "I'm concerned about what others might think of me if they knew about the clutter in my house," and "I have to move things in order to accomplish tasks in my home" are ranked as "strongly disagree" to "strongly agree". For me, inviting a new client to take this short assessment not only establishes a baseline, but is an effective way to start the conversation about why they need assistance, guidance, and support in their organizing efforts. It's also a way to keep that conversation going.

Before you read this book, please take a moment to review the CQLS and take the short quiz. If you're someone who would like to have more order and organization in your life, this short assessment can help you determine how clutter affects your life right now, where you are. Your results can help you set goals regarding how you'd like to change and where you'd like to be. The scale is also an excellent way to begin assessing which of the many approaches in this book might be best for you. Finally, this tool can act as a communication path between you and your therapist, partner, and friends by providing concrete analysis that will help you set a course of action to achieve freedom from the burden of your stuff.

If you're an allied mental health provider, or a friend or partner to someone you feel might be hoarding, have a shopping addiction, or otherwise have too much stuff to be happy, you can also take this quiz; however, make it about *you*, not about the person you're reading this book for. If we don't have our own views and perspectives about our personal situation and environment, it's more difficult to have a point of reference when our clients, friends, and partners rate their own quality of life.

You can access the quiz on the ICD website, under the "Resources" tab.

ABOUT THE METHODS

I n our office, we often get calls from well-meaning and emotionally exhausted family members who are worried about their mother, sister, father, brother, or grandparent. They sometimes even call about neighbors and friends who they fear will lose their home if local authorities discover the state of their living conditions. We listen to the concerned caller and kindly explain that, unless the person suffering from hoarding disorder or chronic disorganization is willing to work with us voluntarily, the chances for creating change in the environment will most likely not be successful.

Our clients who call for themselves might not be ready to receive our help when they call us the first time. Often, they want to find out about our services, get some pricing, and gain information about how we work. Usually, they'll spend some time thinking about whether they're able to begin the process before they can follow through with services. I've worked with clients who have called me, taken down my information, and then waited years to get started. Even after the process begins, there are times when appointments are canceled, rescheduled, or postponed until the client feels "more ready." That's when I say, "It's okay. ***I'm right here*** when you're ready to begin again."

Clutter can be defined with a popular quote by Barbara Hemphill, professional organizer and author of *Taming the Paper Tiger*. Hemphill says that clutter is just "postponed decisions." I agree, but I try not to use *clutter* to describe my client's possessions. It can be a very minimizing term, one that suggests one's belongings have no value, that the items are junk. Only after a client and I work together to make decisions regarding the value of each possession will we make the determination of whether an object is clutter or something special that needs to remain in the person's life and home.

It's up to the individual to seek help, accept assistance, and create the change they want to see in themselves and in their environment. As POs, we can notice, then gently challenge behaviors, habits, and choices, but we can't control a client's path toward a more organized life. We can only be a supportive guide along the way. The following sections outline the different approaches and methods available to us in our efforts to establish and maintain successful working relationships.

METHOD 1

HANDS-ON ORGANIZING ONE-ON-ONE WITH A PROFESSIONAL ORGANIZER

Hands-on organizing is exactly what its name implies and is the most common method of addressing a clutter-filled home. It typically begins with the informal phone assessment.

The Initial Phone Call or the Intake Call

During the initial telephone exchange, the PO learns what the potential client would like to accomplish. We actively listen during most of this call, which ideally lasts fifteen minutes but can go much longer. If the PO feels that the client is going to benefit from his or her services, fees are explained and expectations are discussed. Then an appointment is made for the initial consultation at the client's home or office. Let's explore how this process works in greater depth by meeting our first featured PO, Linda Samuels.

Linda is a PO who works primarily with clients who have chronic disorganization (CD). Linda, an ICD Master Trainer and past president of the organization, has completed all five levels of education that ICD offers since she joined in 2002.

She carefully screens her clients to make sure they're a good match for her. She has gotten better at this process over the years. "Maybe after listening to them," she says, "I discover that it doesn't always have to be *me* that will help them. I try to understand what it is they need." During that initial phone call, she assesses the ability for her and her client to communicate. "If I am not grasping what they are saying, and the rapport is not there, it will not get better if they hire me." In these instances, Linda, who has been organizing professionally since 1992, may recommend a colleague or refer the client to the NAPO website for a better match.

"Right from the get-go, the clients that I was attracted to and that sought me out were those struggling with CD. I never got a call that asked me if I could come and just organize a closet," she explains. "Those were NOT the calls I was getting. Little did I know at the time, but I was going to get involved with my clients in a much longer-term way than I ever imagined. I love the challenge of working with them. And I was interested in the journey. I wanted to help people who couldn't see where they were going. They were the ones that needed help." She knows instinctively that she can help her clients by building a strong relationship with them.

"When you are involved in someone's life in that way, we need to understand that they are going to be on a trajectory course like everyone else but will need more help navigating these times than others."

Linda is a patient person by nature and is very comfortable working in a certain amount of turmoil. "For me," she explains, "I DO like a challenge. I don't want just mindless work. I need my work to require energy, compassion, and creativity."

Linda admits that it takes some people longer than others to be ready for the organizing process. "Change does not happen rapidly with CD clients," Linda states, adding that rarely does it happen that any of her clients are able to make fast changes. She sometimes works with them with her focus on "priming the pump," and then slowly lets clients get ready for the bigger changes that are coming. The overwhelming feeling usually comes from having too much clutter and too many obligations. "All of it," she explains, "involves letting go."

Jonda Beattie, M.Ed., shares how she handles calls inquiring about her organizing services. "Sometimes, I think it is as much of what you don't say as to what you do say. I do a lot more listening than talking. I never assume anything, nor do I ever push for them to make a decision now. I let them know that there is no judgment being made and that we all have our stories. I may ask them why they called me at this time, and I let them talk. I let them ask me questions. I have a template that I use for the intake, but most of it gets filled out without me asking more than a couple of questions about the why and the why now. I do ask them if they have been to my website as that shows a lot about me. I also reassure them that if we work together, they are totally in charge and that they have the final say-so as to what happens with everything they own."

Diane Quintana, a PO who is also an ICD Master Trainer, sometimes gets calls from a mental health practitioner. "Most of my inquiries either begin as an email or as a referral from a therapist. If it is through email, I usually get some information—enough to know if the next step is for the person to ask me more questions in an email or if they are eager to have me call them. Contacting a professional organizer is a HUGE leap of faith for someone who is overwhelmed by clutter and disorganization. Often they are really down on themselves to the point of being almost hopeless. If I can give them a tiny glimmer of hope, kindness, reassurance that help from me (and most professional organizers) is nonjudgmental, then that encourages them to make the next step of scheduling either a virtual or in-person meeting."

Feelings you might have before, during, and after calling a Professional Organizer for the first time:

- Guilt
- Excitement
- Relief
- Anger
- Determination
- Embarrassment
- Denial
- Elation
- Annoyance
- Hope
- Agitation
- Shame
- Overwhelm
- Anxiety

Behaviors you may exhibit as a result of anticipation of the first session with a Professional Organizer:

- Isolating more than usual inside the home
- Socializing more than usual outside the home
- Impulsively tidying up and shifting piles around to "clean up" before the organizer arrives
- Irritability and acting out some uncomfortable emotions towards others
- Avoidance that could result in canceling and rescheduling the session

It's all right to cancel. It's okay to reschedule. *We are here when YOU are ready.* Just as there's no judgment from us in how your home looks, there are no hard feelings when we receive cancellations.

Clients have reported feeling a sense of relief after contacting me for the first time. I've had clients tell me that they could actually hear my empathy and gentle nature in my voice. Our conversations made them feel safe and at ease.

I remember this same feeling after leaving my therapist's office after the first visit. I had found her contact information on the *Psychology Today* website directory or therapists in my area for Cognitive Behavioral Therapy (CBT). I had been feeling somewhat depressed and anxious, and then when it came to a head for me, I felt desperate for the answers—for the help. I had let my negative feelings go unchecked for way too long, and it was time for a professional to step in.

When I got into my car after leaving her office that day, I felt as though I had just opened a pressure valve in my body. I had been carrying around so many heavy rocks in a backpack that only I could see for quite some time. I think my therapist might have felt like I was spraying a firehose full of angry Chihuahuas at her every week, but better at her than my family, friends, and work team! When it all gets too heavy for me to carry anymore, she's there to listen and share the tools to make my life easier to manage. The fears are less terrifying and the moments of accomplishments actually celebrated, even small ones. My sadness can't be erased like I had hoped, but I can bear it. And that's key for me. This is coincidentally how my clients report feeling after each weekly session with me or a member our organizing team.

Here's one thing for certain that will happen once a Professional Organizer is hired: your life will change.

There will be a shift in awareness of the way the items in the home will be viewed, approached, and handled. There will be some discomfort as difficult decisions are made to discard, donate, sell, or keep possessions that up until now were part of the everyday home atmosphere. Even if the initial assessment is all that gets accomplished at first, that's still useful. It's still a new insight that wasn't there before. If, during that initial assessment, a written plan is developed and provided, it's yet another tool to use when ready to commit further to the process, independently or with the PO. And maybe that change, that small, tiny shift, is enough for now.

If our clients are open to even one visit, we can make a difference. We won't minimize what our clients feel is important. What we WILL do is talk to our clients about what kind of home environment they wish to have and create a plan with them, complete with achievable steps, dates for any phases, in order of priority. We will then walk beside our clients as they step through their goals, one at a time, at a pace that works for them, gently challenging them when it's safe to do so and being professionally present during emotionally charged sessions.

Initial Organizing Assessment

This face-to-face visit is crucial for the PO to understand the true scope of services required and to establish a bond with the client. During that critical first hour, the PO needs to build trust with the client and make sure the relationship is a good fit. The client will be evaluating the PO's reaction to their home as well as listening to and contemplating the validity and feasibility of the solutions offered.

The initial visit usually includes a tour of the home or, at minimum, the spaces that need the most attention. Sharing a private home (and its contents) with a stranger is never easy, especially when the client may feel trepidation, vulnerability, and shame regarding their home's condition. There are also areas that the client may not feel comfortable sharing just yet, or ever. The PO does everything she or he can to create a nonjudgmental atmosphere to make it possible for the client to communicate their challenges, discuss what they have tried in the past, and talk about their hopes for a better way of managing their life. It's an emotional time, and the PO empathetically understands the courage it takes for the client to make that initial phone call and allow the PO into the sanctuary of their home.

In some cases, the PO will create a written and somewhat detailed organizing plan and share it with the client. This is a highly individualized, customized plan for the client. It can include plans for addressing the physical space as well as for changing the client's daily habits and practices. Goals are discussed and set during this meeting, and some ground rules and expectations will be agreed to by both parties. An example of a ground rule might be that all magazines published prior to a certain year will be recycled after the client has inspected the pile. Another example would be that anything in a certain category, such as books, be grouped together for review, and any that are damaged or not repairable will be discarded. Some POs prioritize the spaces to be addressed based on the client's wishes. Some will also design a plan that begins with clearing a storage area, such as a garage. Once a storage space like this is cleared, it can be used as a temporary location for items leaving from other parts of the house.

Once the PO and the client agree that they're compatible and that the PO's services will be helpful, the two will schedule future organizing sessions. This happens before the PO leaves the client that first day. My team and I always schedule at least one date in the near future and usually three.

The First Organizing Session

The PO will arrive on time. Not early and never late. Often, if I arrive too early, I'll park down the road a bit, check emails, make calls, or meditate before I drive on to the client's house. I don't appreciate it when guests arrive too early to my house (I'm always making last-minute preparations), so it's unfair for me to show up earlier than expected at a client's house, especially the first time we work together.

The PO will bring a tote bag. I call mine and those belonging to our team members a workbag. It usually contains these items:

- Tape measure
- Five to ten manila file folders
- Permanent markers of different thicknesses
- Roll of packing tape
- Label maker, refill cartridges, and batteries
- Scissors
- Box cutter
- Small roll of garbage bags
- Notebook and pen (or tablet)
- Snack(s) and water bottle

I usually keep my bag with me at all times during the organizing session, because I need the items in it fairly frequently. Some POs wear a tool belt, which allows them to grab what they need quickly.

I make it a practice to stop periodically and midway through the session to check in with my client and make sure they're doing all right emotionally and physically. I remind them to drink some water, tea, or coffee and take short breaks. Their self-care during the organizing process is key. Sorting and making decisions about the contents of a home is an emotional and tiring process. Releasing objects that have been a part of someone's life isn't easy. Just ask anyone who has ever moved. Legitimate parting with one's pieces of history occurs naturally when home transitions are made. However, when someone needs help to declutter for a purpose other than moving, the reasons are compelling in their own right.

During this first session, which usually runs two to three hours, the PO and the client learn a lot about each other. The PO discovers the best way to communicate with and support the client as they sort, decide on, and dispatch items. Every client experience is different, but when the fit is right between a PO and a client, the rhythm of activities becomes smooth, easy, and even fun. Some clients like to play music while we sort, and they begin relaxing about the process when progress becomes more visible. When the labeled sorting bins I bring start filling up with opened mail, unopened mail, office supplies, receipts, and multiple other categories, there seems to be a shift—a quiet exhale of relief from my clients, a belief that getting organized is actually attainable. The first step has been taken, and that's worth celebrating. About fifteen minutes before the session ends, the PO lets the client know it's almost time to finish up and begins to tidy up the workspace. The PO and client review the plan and confirm or set the next appointment.

If the client has made decisions to donate items and has agreed that the PO may take them to a donation center, the PO loads his or her car with those items, clarifying whether a donation slip and itemized list are desired. If the client prefers to take the items to the donation center personally, the PO will help load their car. The third option is to designate a space—a room or even a corner of the home—to hold items to be donated. The PO or the client can arrange for a local charity to pick up the items. Not all clients are comfortable with having many discarded possessions out on their porch for their neighbors to see. In those cases, smaller collections (four to five bags or boxes) may be set out at a time until all the items are gone.

Checking in after the first session is a good practice. The PO can confirm the next appointment and also see how the client is doing. This goes a long way to building a relationship of communication and care.

The Second and Subsequent Organizing Sessions

During the next session, the client and the PO strive to develop a rhythm within the organizing space. At the beginning of the session, the PO may present the written plan for review before work commences and check in with the client to see how they feel after the first session. If this sounds like a therapy session, there's a good reason. Often, POs, while not clinicians, are helping their client much like a therapist or social worker would. There are parallels: letting the client share their stories, their fears, and their hopes of having a better life; giving the client tools to cope with their environment and possessions; and helping the client navigate the emotional consequences of sifting through memories, old bills, paper stacks, and abandoned projects. The process can be emotionally draining. The PO doesn't actually offer any clinical or therapeutic advice but may encourage their client to reach out to a therapist or mental health professional.

Session length is usually set by the client and the PO and depends on the ability of the client to focus on the task at hand. For example, some clients are open to working four hours at a time, with a short break here and there, on an area that has easier decisions to make, such as a corner of the basement, which may hold items they haven't seen in a long time. The clients I've worked with have usually been more amenable to working on ridding their home of passive items (objects they no longer use) versus active items (items in their immediate living and sleeping spaces) that they see every day. Sometimes I offer a "mix-it-up" session. For clients who struggle with paper piles, two hours may be just right for sorting those. Then we add forty-five minutes of decluttering a pantry to finish the session. This offers the client a change of scenery and some respite from tougher decisions, and we're still meeting the client's goals.

Session length can increase over time, sometimes in increments as small as fifteen minutes per session. At my company, we try to work with our clients for at least two hours but not more than six. This maximum-length guideline is important. We believe that after six hours (four, really), our clients are so mentally and emotionally exhausted that the quality of their decision-making diminishes and they face burnout.

One of the strongest benefits of in-person appointments is that we're able to be our client's arms and legs. If a client decides they need something from another room, the PO will usually fetch it. If a bundle of clothes needs to go to donation, the PO will bag it, record it, and put it by the door to go out. If a basement shelf is empty and needs to be wiped down before new items are placed there, the PO will not only wipe down the shelf but will also contain and label the new items to be placed there. These actions allow the client to stay focused and maintain their momentum so that they have a successful session.

As with the first session, we allow fifteen minutes at the end of this session to tidy up our workspace, load cars with donations or items to sell, if appropriate, and make or confirm future appointments.

Sessions can be emotional. Linda Samuels relates to her clients in many ways and sometimes, she says, what's happening with a client could also be happening in her own life. "It could be that close," she shares. "But I can give them the gift of my attention. We (Professional Organizers) give our clients that. This is rare for them to receive, and I feel like this is a part of my job, my responsibility to them." Linda mentions that she uses her "mirror neurons" to sense when she's feeling the same as a client is feeling during a session. "I will feel it. I will stop, acknowledge it, and sit with it. I don't wash the feelings away, in either of us." Recently while she was at a client's home, the client's caregiver announced the death of the client's husband. Linda sat with her client patiently and supportively that day.

There are boundaries that Linda adheres to as well, lines that she teeters on with each client, and it's not the same with all clients. When asked how far she pushes without pushing too far, Linda says her technique is to state the goals up front but stay fluid with the process. "What are they willing to do? We don't want to *make* them do anything, but encouraging them profusely works for me. There is a feel to it—a give and take. I am challenged with sometimes wondering if I pushed them a little more, then they would be able to move faster. It is really hard to push someone through their emotions, so we have to be gentle with them. If there is resistance, I will back off. I will let them lead. *I will not take over.*"

From helping clients cope with their daily lives to simply locating an important piece of paper, Linda feels that she helps her clients at a core level. "The parts of their lives that I can help them with makes a big difference in how they handle the other parts," she shares. She feels that helping people have little wins among the losses gives them one less stress that they have to deal with. "It's not uncommon for me to walk into a situation where a client is in distress. My goal is that they are in a different place by the end of the session. They are laughing, they are smiling, they are *better*."

Jonda Beattie often shares some of her own story with a client. "I will also let them know that many others walk similar paths, although each person is unique. I remind them that they are special.

"I keep them motivated when working through the process by each time having them share their wins since the last session. I will often add to their win list from things I have heard them say like, 'I did not get the clothes put away that were on the loveseat but instead I cleared out a drawer and spent some time with my daughter.' I will turn that into two wins. 'You cleaned out a drawer that will now make more space for your clothes, and you prioritized your time to allow time with your daughter.'"

Jonda also takes the time to remind clients of their vision for the project and point out what they're doing to work toward that vision. "Nonjudgmental encouragement and accountability seem to go a long way," she says.

METHOD 2

HANDS-ON ORGANIZING WITH A PROFESSIONAL ORGANIZING TEAM

Working with a professional organizing team has many similarities to the in-person one-on-one sessions. The main reason a client chooses the team method is that they have a large area they need to address in a short period of time. I've had clients ask for a team of four people to tackle a large two-car garage in two days, six hours each, because they only have two days off work and need to get the most done in the short amount of time they have.

Some clients request a large organizing team because they enjoy having a group around them. They feel more supported and get a lot of undivided attention. Extroverts who live alone or with just one person get recharged by being around people, and organizing teams can provide that positive energy boost.

The Initial Phone Call or the Intake Call

This call is similar to the call explained for Method 1. The PO and the client go over options and determine which method is better suited for the client (and project) success. If the client understands and agrees with the fees involved for a team of at least two POs, the client and PO will set an appointment for the initial organizing assessment.

Initial Organizing Assessment

The lead PO will arrive at the house, usually with an additional PO from their team, to meet the client, discuss goals, and tour the home or areas to be organized. A plan will be developed with dates for goal achievement, and ground rules regarding expectations and criteria for keeping versus releasing items will be established.

The First Organizing Session

Upon arrival at the home, the lead PO will gather the entire team, including the client, and review the day's objectives in a sort of team huddle. Materials will be unloaded and placed in each work area. These may be small cardboard boxes, plastic totes (ranging in size), and bags for donation or trash. Each PO usually carries their own workbag filled with the tools they need to work efficiently.

Specific tasks are assigned to each team member. The lead PO will usually work with the client and guide the process for the day's work. The rest of the team conducts sorting activities, such as presorting items in one room in preparation for the client's review. This likely will include labeling piles with recommendations like "to decide," "to recycle," "to discard," or "to donate."

When team members have completed their assigned tasks, they'll check in with the lead PO to see if there are other areas that they can begin working in. At this time, the lead PO will assess whether to take the client to the areas the team has presorted or to continue doing the work they're already in the middle of. If the lead PO decides to have the client review what has been sorted, the other team member(s) can:

- follow the lead PO and client to the sorted area to assist with suggested actions, such as bagging and boxing items going to be donated and recording them for tax purposes.
- stay behind in the area where the lead PO and client have been working to tidy up, box items for donation or sale, and organize what the client has decided to keep. The team member will know what goes where from verbal explanations and notes or signs left on stacks of objects.
- split up (if there are more than two extra team members). One can follow and assist the client and the lead PO, and the other can contain designated items in the area where the lead PO and client have been working.

The Second and Subsequent Organizing Sessions

The next sessions will most likely mirror the first. Depending on budget and the volume of items to be sorted and dispatched, the team composition could stay the same, increase, or decrease.

Progress is likely more noticeable when a team is involved. When the client decides to let go of an item, a team member can remove it immediately, making progress more visible. A PO sometimes takes photographs to show the client how much space is opening up. I often share with a client how far they've come, even if the area opened up is one square foot of space.

The team approach also adds a sense of camaraderie to the organizing environment, even in the most somber of occasions. Janine Adams of Peace of Mind Organizing keeps it as fun as she can. "We really try to make the organizing process fun to the extent possible. That helps them stay motivated. When I plug into the client's sense of humor so that the process isn't deadly serious, it tends to keep them coming back for more. In addition, I always talk with the clients about their goals and their vision for what their space (and their life) will be like after they have finished. When I sense that their motivation is flagging, we can discuss their goals and how they imagine feeling. Sometimes that will reinvigorate them."

When we were filming an episode of *Hoarders* (Season 11, A&E Network) in October of 2019, the client, Sherry, came to call our team "her girls." She felt a sisterhood had developed between the four of us, and she was right. Through the hours and days of this dramatic project, Sherry came to trust us and relied on us to meet the deadline the show had set. The director also wanted our team to make sure the client complied willingly with the process we established, as the psychiatrist had reinforced the idea that this was voluntary on her part. Sherry cried angry and sorrowful tears on our shoulders, took little walks with each of us, and received hugs whenever she needed one. On the last day, we joined hands in the early morning before the cameras rolled. Choking back tears, Sherry looked at all of us and said, "My angels, I know you are with me today." Crew members on our junk-hauling team, G.I. Haul, became our brothers-in-arms. We worked side by side with them each day to rid the house of decades of items she no longer wanted. Sherry told our team how much she appreciated all of us and the men's hard work to fill the dumpsters and hauling trucks.

Janine Adams only works with her clients if they're willing to take a team approach. For new clients who are CD, she manages their expectations well. She says straightforwardly, "This is how I work. I lead teams. I do not take on one-on-one clients. If I feel that they require that, I refer to my colleague, Denise Lee, or to one of my own independent contractors." Janine operates with a team of three POs, including herself. "I still have clients that I work with one-on-one, but they are former clients."

A recent project involved helping a former pro bono client who had a few months to live. When the client first reached out in 2010, Janine ascertained that she didn't have much money. "I was giving an organizing talk near her house the week after we had that initial call and asked her to come to it to learn for free. The next thing I knew, I was putting together a big ol' team, and we began helping her to get organized." The most recent contact with the client had a different mission to it altogether. "She wanted to make her last months more pleasant, and so we had five or six sessions before she passed away." The intimacy of being in that sacred space in that short window of time before her death was emotionally satisfying and challenging. "She was such a lovely woman, and it was great to help her." After the client passed away, Janine and fellow PO Denise Lee helped her friends clean out her apartment. "That was very sad," she admits.

METHOD 3

BRAIN-BASED SPECIALTY ORGANIZING AND COACHING

So far, we have addressed what it is like to work with a PO in a one-on-one traditional organizing project, as well as with a team. We'll now explore what it's like to work with a PO who specializes in working with clients who have a brain-based disorder such as ADHD. These sessions are typically one-on-one so that the PO and client can focus all their energy and attention on the session's objectives. I'll also introduce collaborative therapy, which is a team approach involving the client, a therapist, and the PO.

Initial Call and Initial Organizing Consultation

These early consultations may go a bit longer than those for a client not challenged by a brain-based disorder. This is due in part to the necessity for gathering more information and diving deeper into what the client feels is causing the disorganization in their lives. Clients are often surprised to hear that the PO they've hired has a history of, or is currently living with, their own brain-based challenge.

Sue West, CPO-CD, MHC, is the former president of ICD and recently earned her master's degree in Mental Health Counseling. She works full time as an adult clinician at a community mental health center in New Hampshire. Prior to being a therapist, she was a professional organizer and an ADHD coach. Sue identified early on in her organizing career that she belonged in the world of helping those with chronic disorganization because it was "about the psychology and the emotions, and I thought I really need to understand more about this. I was inspired by my colleagues at ICD conferences but also by my clients. It's really chronic disorganization that is beginning to get in their way every day. They may say to themselves, 'I know I have this great potential, but I'm not achieving it.'"

Sue delved further into coaching those with ADHD and became an industry leader in the field, subsequently publishing a workbook. She then went on to write a publication for ICD for mental health professionals about how to work with POs who are educated in ADHD. When Sue realized that more and more of her organizing clients were saying, "This is better than seeing a therapist," she realized she was headed toward integrating therapy into her practice with her clients in some way.

Sue often shared her own story of living with ADHD with her clients when it was appropriate and openly in her publications. "So many people that have chronic disorganization and have brain-based challenges are often isolated and fragile, mentally. They have some type of mental health issue going on, everything from ADHD to hoarding to anxiety. It is all very complex. Collaborative therapy is a really positive and supportive way to help someone with a brain-based challenge to sustain success with the skills they have learned with a coach or professional organizer."

Collaborative therapy has always been a winning strategy for Sue's clients, and now that she's a therapist, she spends the majority of her time working in her office. Therapists typically don't go into homes and treat clients for their mental health issues. In fact, while most agencies offer some type of functional support service staff who go into homes to teach skills and do some type of organizing with them, there are still many therapists who aren't aware of what a professional organizer, trained in CD, could do for their clients. "Sometimes, the staff person going into the homes doesn't understand why the stuff keeps coming back," Sue shared. "The staff person may be able to organize for or with a client but might not be able to teach and train a client how to really learn to be organized, which actually eases mental health symptoms. A Professional Organizer could accompany the visiting agency staff member to help the client in the home to learn more about *how to organize* with a sustainable system in place, and to address why there is backsliding after so much effort is made to clear clutter from the home. The Professional Organizer and agency staff member would ideally work together to record the progress and techniques, as well as the therapeutic approach so that documentation compliance standards can be met."

Alice Price, the "Long Island Organizer," started her organizing business in 2000 after only one year of retirement from her long career in information technology. "I read an article in the newspaper about adults with ADHD. It said that these adults can be helped with the assistance of a professional organizer." Alice had raised a son who was diagnosed with ADHD in the 1980s. "The attitude towards ADHD then was just to 'get over it, just do it.'" Alice admits that the lack of understanding of the diagnosis was challenging for her as a mother trying to help her son to learn.

"From day ONE," Alice says of beginning her education and training for professional organizing, "it was a feeling of being at home. These people spoke my language and understood things I would say. When I was organizing, I was helping people, and it all just came together. It wasn't until I was working with my third client when I realized I was working in a hoarded house. I did not know at the time that was that it was. I have this skill, this talent to organize, but there is a *whole lot more* to it than that. ICD came along, and there were these people who taught me how to deal with all of that. The education I was receiving was so enlightening to me, and also to my son, who was grown at that point."

Alice, a CPO-CD and COC, has indeed learned a lot since embarking on her career, not only from her clients, but also with formal learning through her member associations. She has a specialist certificate in hoarding and ADD as well as in chronic disorganization.

"I enjoy learning new things. With ICD, there are always new classes, new material. I am constantly adding new tools to my toolbox. To do this after all of these years in business is incredible. We are continuously adding skills to ourselves and to our clients."

Alice especially likes introducing physical tools to help people with their everyday life challenges, like going from digital to analog clocks. "People have been struggling with time [management] their whole lives, and to teach them to use something like the Time Timer opens up a whole new world for them and sharing this joy is wonderful, and that's why I do this." The Time Timer is a small analog timer that shows the user exactly how much time they have remaining on a task or activity. POs use these with clients who have difficulty finishing tasks due to ADD or who struggle with other challenges that make activities seem overwhelming.

Alice's prospective clients can look at her website and know who she wants to help. Alice said that she hopes people look at her services with hope. "They say to themselves, 'She is going to help me figure it out. She isn't going to tell me to just do it.' It's not easy to reach out for help."

Comorbidity, or the coexistence of more than one disorder in one person, is common with Alice's clients. "People that have

ADHD call me, looking for help with time management, and we end up working on their ADHD issues. A lot of my clients come from a dysfunctional family and have low self-esteem. My clients who have ADHD will often have that paired with a new diagnosis, like anxiety."

Therapy is important. Alice prefers that her clients with comorbidity, or with any singular disorder—hoarding, ADHD, anxiety—are in therapy while she works with them. Her typical client has already been in therapy, has had a breakthrough or epiphany, and now is ready to start getting rid of their stuff. If they don't have a therapist and rely on Alice's professional expertise only, Alice guides them to seek treatment by gently telling them that they need more help than she can give them. When collaborative therapy happens, she's happy to participate. "One of my clients wanted me to speak to her therapist, and while we were meeting all together, he referred to her client and said, 'You're helping her.' He saw progress."

"It's very personal." Alice sees the deeper emotional effects of the organizing session. "Sometimes, my clients' families are unsupportive for one reason or another. It's very easy to be absorbed into their situations. One of my challenges is when they are telling me stories, I can get pulled into them. They need to talk, and they need to be heard, but we have to get some work done too." Naturally, her clients turn to her for clinical advice, which she gently redirects. She says to them, "That's really interesting that you say that. Have you ever talked to your therapist about that?" Alice credits her training at ICD for learning the words and phrases to use successfully with her clients when the boundaries get blurry.

"The real value of working with these clients is emotional, not just getting their space back. That is the beginning of turning that self-esteem around. I give them something they never had before—help. They suddenly see themselves as capable."

"I think I always attracted people that were messy," says Cris Sgrott, an ICD Master Trainer, PO, and organizer coach. Cris utilizes both a team and a one-on-one approach with her clients who have hoarding tendencies and CD. A former renovation specialist, she started her business in 2007 when she realized she was drawn to people who needed her help to get order in their homes and lives. "Give me a complex person with a challenge and I will thrive! Our clients come to the table as functional human beings that have lived this amazing life. They just want to stop struggling and live like 'other people,'" she says.

Cris defines her ideal client as someone who really wants to change. "I appreciate the journey too—even with those who aren't sure what they wanted. When the light comes on, they can really shine and realize what it is that they hired you for. I already feel that I am a good listener. I am interested in them and how they show up to the world. In coaching you learn to let them have their space and let them talk about themselves with validation from me. It feels like I am dating all the time!

It's a new relationship and I treat it that way. I am a much better listener because of coaching."

Denise Lee, a CPO and organizer coach, has a bachelor's degree in psychology, as well as many certificates in brain-based studies from ICD. She started her company, Clear Spaces, in 2005.

While the focus of the organizing session needs to be what the client wants, Denise points out that as a coach, her job is also to shift that focus onto goals by pointing out what isn't working. "I say, 'This situation might be your problem, but I am here to help you think it through. Let's brainstorm together!' It is so important for me to really listen to the client, because sometimes what they say they want isn't what they might *need* right now."

Denise was hired to organize the whole house of a woman who had recently gone through major life changes. They developed the organizing plan together, and during the first session, the client stated that she would like to start organizing the kitchen, because it was the heart of the home and that's where she "should" begin. However, when the client walked past a large pile of stuff—approximately five feet high by five feet wide—in the living room, she became visibly flustered. "I said, 'Yes, your kitchen *is* the heart of the home, but let me throw this out there: Why don't we start with the pile in the living room?' I could see that it was really such a drain on her by the way she walked past it. She was initially hesitant and said that it was such an 'icky' pile, but acquiesced. Two and a half hours later, the pile was GONE. She began to do a little Snoopy happy dance and was genuinely so pleased that she had regained that corner of her home. The bigger thing that she had done was to truly tackle the thing that had been really eating at her, and she is so much more in control now."

With brain-based challenged individuals, there can be setbacks. To offset these, Denise checks in more frequently with her clients who are at risk of backsliding in between organizing sessions. But what about when the work during a session gets challenging for a client suffering from mental health issues? Denise stops the session upon noticing the behavior and encourages a reboot. "You know what? This is a crap day for you, isn't it? Your amygdala is on overdrive! We are going to stop right here. Go do something fun today and recharge your battery. I will see you for our next appointment."

Denise's clients who are in collaborative therapy while getting organized have an ally on their side. "Part of my training through ICD has made me more effective in working with therapists too. With permission, I can share what I am noticing and working on with the client that the therapist might not be aware of, because the client may not be sharing how things are really going in the home environment, and the therapist is not in the trenches with the client like I am. They might be asked about how their paper organizing is going, and the client will say 'fine,' but I am noticing that the client is really struggling with a collection of recipes that have significant emotional meaning. I will say, 'Things can be really rough when we are in the client's papers.' This way the issues can be addressed in therapy sooner than later and spur on some real progress for the client."

Denise works with individuals who have ADD, bipolar disorder, anxiety disorder, sleep disorders, and schizophrenia. While these diagnoses carry several challenges for her clients, she sees the clutter as just one aspect of their lives. "My clients who have really struggled with hoarding or CD are just people! They are interesting, fascinating. The clients I work with are very nice people—kind, considerate, trying hard to do well in this world. Their issues with clutter are not who they are. They have a mark on their life, and they are miserable because of it. This work is gratifying because I get to be a part of the solution."

METHOD 4

VIRTUAL PROFESSIONAL ORGANIZING AND COACHING

Virtual organizing or coaching involves the client calling the virtual organizer (VO) or coach directly or using an online meeting platform, such as Skype or Zoom, to conduct sessions. Like in-person sessions, these are geared to help clients become more successful at managing their days, their relationships, and their home and work environments.

Sheila Delson, PO and president of Free Domain Concepts, LLC, raised two sons in the seventies. Her older son had dyslexia and ADD, and her second son was diagnosed with ADHD. She was told both sons had a brain deficit. "I have always been intuitive and knew that this could be improved upon. I worked really closely with their special education teachers to find a way to help them learn." These teachers saw in Sheila what she describes as "a firm interest" and asked her to take a volunteer position as a child advocate for children with learning disabilities. She remembers going away for five days to train on how to fulfill this important role, including how to develop an Individualized Education Program (IEP) for each child in her charge.

Sheila began organizing professionally in the early 90s and was inspired by Stephanie Culp's book, *How to Conquer Clutter*. She joined NAPO and followed the work and career of Judith Kolberg. Her stalwart belief is that people who think differently from the norm are "still very capable, intelligent, and have enormous potential despite learning differently." Sheila began as most POs do, providing services on site, organizing homes, offices, and schedules with her clients. It wasn't long before she began working with the population of clients with CD. It was a natural progression for Sheila to begin working with those who have chronic learning disabilities. "I was always attracted to this kind of work," Sheila admitted. "I believe I organically saw the need for me to be helping this population."

Sheila, cofounder of the Institute for Challenging Disorganization and cocreator of the Clutter-Hoarding Scale®, currently offers a virtual program that allows her to transition from working physically with her clients to coaching them one-on-one over the phone or using virtual means like Skype or Zoom. She also offers training, mentoring, and certification for experienced POs who would like to offer virtual professional organizing services to their clients.

Sheila wants to see the industry expand beyond the traditional one-to-one learning experience. She feels that there's a widening gap between clients who can afford our services and clients who can't. Virtual organizing, for Sheila, bridges that gap. She would love to see our services be less costly and more accessible and available.

"The industry has become so super-niched that we are only serving a small population. This work is my passion. The 'higher needy' are our challenging disorganization clientele, unable to participate in society due to mental health issues that block them from engaging in the world. My mission is to teach these individuals to handle themselves independently, financially, managing their own lives the best way possible, creating routines based in self-discipline. We are obligated as professionals to fix this."

Virtual Professional Organization is a growing trend in the organizing industry. Vickie Dellaquila, CPO, CPO-CD, and CVPO (Certified Virtual Professional Organizer) says, "I always ask my clients about their different issues that they are having and ask them the length of time that they have been dealing with it. I listen for a long time. When they are talking, a common thread appears. They say, 'I just can't seem to do it on my own.'" While Vickie uses Zoom to conduct sessions, she receives photos and other information about a client's environment digitally before she begins work. "We always discuss the goals that they want to achieve and outline together how we are going to get there."

Vickie didn't always use virtual organizing as her method to help those struggling with CD or hoarding. She began professional organizing after a career as a case worker in a nursing home, where she saw the need for seniors to downsize before coming into the nursing home. "I saw in social services that there were people that had no ability to manage their finances, their stuff, their lives, so I started a budgeting program at North Hills Community Outreach where I worked."

After founding Organization Rules, Inc. in 2002, it took Vickie about eight years to realize she preferred to work with seniors who hoarded and were chronically disorganized. After receiving more education through ICD, she began to work strictly with that clientele and created a Clutter Support class. She also taught caregivers and the general public how to recognize and find support for this unique population. In 2020, Vickie's business went almost completely virtual.

Vickie recognizes several benefits to virtual organizing, with the most popular being the time factor. "This method of organizing works well for people who have limited time. We meet once per week for a minimum of one hour, so it doesn't have to be a long session." Another reason for virtual organizing's appeal is its lack of intrusiveness. Sometimes people aren't ready to have someone in their home. Still another plus is the affordability. The cost for virtual sessions can be considerably lower. Some VOs charge less per hour for their time, because they don't have the costs of time and travel to a client's home.

Virtual organizing clients are often assigned manageable tasks in between sessions. These could be anything from finishing the sort through a small pile of paper or the objects in one closet to taking items to a donation center. Vickie follows up with the client during the next session or checks in with them in between to see if they did their homework. This helps drive up accountability, but not everyone can make good on their promises. Then Vickie uses the "Body-Doubling" technique. "If there are boxes in the room that have to be addressed, I ask [the client] to go and look in the box with me. They take the laptop, tablet, or phone with them, and they open the box with me 'there.' I am with them as they pull items out and go through them with me. Body-Doubling works. It's a support. This can be just as successful as hands-on organizing." Body-Doubling is used by POs in person as well as virtually.

There are some POs in this book who are also certified as Organizer Coaches. Organizer coaches offer virtual sessions, just like POs, but they have a different approach. Instead of the PO doing an assessment and creating the organizing plan for the client, the coach works directly with the client to help the client design the plan themselves, looking carefully at what the client's values are, and long-term desired outcomes.

As with in-person organizing sessions, the success of virtual sessions is dependent upon the client's motivation and commitment to the process. "My clients have to be all-in," Vickie says.

It's important to note that there are circumstances where virtual organizing is not the best solution for a client. Not everyone is able to feel successful connecting virtually with a PO or coach. Some people need the physical presence of another person. If someone is dealing with ADHD, for example, the ability to focus on one area at a time during a session might become even more challenging virtually than it would in-person, even if the coach is highly skilled. Some ADHD clients of mine could only concentrate if I was physically next to them or at a close distance, sorting items using our predetermined "ground rules" and timers. Verbal and physical cues can be extremely helpful to a client during an organizing session. My clients often tell me they "couldn't wait for my energy" to arrive at their home, and I completely understand. There are days when I have an important project due for my business or myself, and I need an "accountability partner" with me to be productive.

Further, some clients are not physically able to carry unwanted items out to be donated—even to their porch. This could be due to a disability, temporary pain, or an illness that prevents them from moving too much or too far, let alone carrying heavy bags or boxes. POs are typically the ones who gather the bags of donated items and place them in a vehicle for drop-off or in the area of the home designated for pick up by a charity.

Sometimes, clients simply don't have the patience or technological skillset to use a computer or tablet to participate in a virtual session. Glitches like internet problems and lost signals can occur, and this can lead to disappointment and unmet goals. The client's frustration with their inability to troubleshoot technology issues also complicates the process, making it less desirable to continue with services.

When virtual organizing is not able to stand alone as the solution to disorganization, a PO may combine it with hands-on organizing. We'll explore that hybrid option next.

METHOD 5

HYBRID ORGANIZING SERVICES

Collaboration between Professional Organizers and Coaches

Hybrid organizing services, as the name suggests, combine hands-on organizing and virtual organizing and coaching. Not all POs have teams in place and are often sole proprietors of their practices. Having a trained group of hands-on organizing experts to call upon allows the client to have the benefits of a full organizing experience. In the hybrid style of organizing, the PO conducts the initial consultation either face-to-face or over the phone and may begin providing organizing or coaching services. Once the need for hands-on services is identified, the PO makes recommendations to the chosen team, and a carefully crafted synergistic plan is put in place.

If a PO or organizer coach is already working hands-on with a client with CD or hoarding disorder, they may realize that the client requires additional assistance or direction. For example, the organizing process may have hit a plateau. To prevent backsliding, the PO and the client might agree that the best way forward is to engage another PO or an organizing coach.

Sue West offered this as a solution in her former coaching practice, so her clients benefitted from her expertise and education and the physical environment still was addressed. She would often receive calls from POs who had hit a wall using "normal strategies" with their client. They knew that, due to a client's brain-based challenges, Sue's coaching services were in order, first to create new strategies. "I liked to pair my services with that of a professional organizing team. I did the coaching and the organizer did the physical work. This is a neat way to empower the client because if they are trying to downsize their house or organize their scrapbook area, this method can work really well. The client and I figured out what the systems and tools were going to be, and then the professional organizer went in and implemented it alone or with a team of other professional organizers."

There are many collaborative ways that two or more POs can work with the same client. Our company, Discover Organizing, provides subcontracted professional labor for a PO in our area. Vickie Dellaquila is a Master Trainer for ICD and works as a solo practitioner. When needed, our team of POs trained to work in the hoarding environment assists her in the home, either alongside her or following a list of tasks that she and her client have decided ahead of time we can complete independently. In the latter scenario, we report back to Vickie what we accomplished and share feedback from the client. This feedback may include the client's wish to receive more guidance from Vickie before proceeding. If that's so, they'll set up a time to work together before we return.

Vickie's passion for helping this population is clear. "I really love what I do, especially when I can see some progress, even a little bit. The clients can feel it; they can see it. It brings me so much joy, even if it is just a little inch forward. Not just them letting go of the stuff, but about the emotions that accompany it." Her perspective shines through in her work. She shares that "Everyone is different, but they all want the same thing—to be wanted, to be cared for, to be loved. I get to be one of those people that gives them that, and it is a privilege. I am grateful that they let me in their lives, into their homes. They are lonely at times. I am grateful for their trust."

Providing support services to fellow POs is rewarding to us because our team not only gets the opportunity to help the client, but we can also learn from someone with the level of education that Vickie has.

The added benefit of hybrid services is the speed and efficiency in which goals can be met. The process runs more quickly than if Vickie was working alone. Collective teamwork is successful in scenarios like this, because the client feels supported by a "village" that circles them with support and care and also gets the job done.

METHOD 6

ORGANIZING CLASSES

Many POs offer online classes, in-person classes, and courses at local community colleges, libraries, and religious buildings. I have taught everything from downsizing, organizing (both home and office), productivity, and photo organizing. There's usually a PO in your area who offers such classes, particularly in the spring and fall when people have the time and the motivation to change their habits.

Now that virtual classes, webinars, and support meetings are available on such online platforms as Zoom, Webex, and Skype, opportunities to learn new skills are more prevalent than ever. POs who use this teaching style will, at times, offer their individual coaching and consultation services after class to interested participants.

Many individuals and organizations offer content-rich online classes, some of which are listed below.

Institute for Challenging Disorganization (ICD)

The ICD website (www.challengingdisorganization.org) offers classes to organizing and mental health professionals as well as to anyone in the general population who is seeking to understand chronic disorganization. The classes cost $39 each for nonsubscribers and range in topics such as:

- Using Self Understanding as a Bridge to Improved Functioning, with Dr. Lesley Cook.
- Managing Productivity and Chronic Disorganization in the Corporate Office Setting, with Clare Kumar.
- Functional Performance in Aging Clients with CD: Using Therapy Insights to Maximize Organizing Results, with Cindy Sullivan, CPO and Tim Sullivan, MS, OTR/L.

The schedule for the classes has been standardized and is as follows:

One-hour live classes are presented at 8:00 p.m. (Eastern Time Zone)

- January–March on Mondays
- April–June on Tuesdays
- July–September on Wednesdays
- October–December on Thursdays

Hoarding Home Solutions

Hoarding Home Solutions is an Australian-based organization providing training and insight into hoarding disorder. Two professionals, Wendy Hanes and Angela Esnouf, have created three separate classes: one for support professionals, one for independent service providers, and one for family and friends of individuals struggling with hoarding disorder. Hoarding Home Solutions intends to bridge the gap between hoarding theory and practice.

Hoarding Home Solutions for Support Professionals

This course is designed to educate social workers, case managers, and other support professionals on the proper techniques and mindset required to work with someone who has hoarding disorder. The course offers twelve modules and additional resources, including access to a private Facebook group and lifetime access to news of discoveries in the field. This course is most effective for people who regularly work with those who have hoarding disorder.

Hoarding Home Solutions for Independent Service Providers

This course is structured to educate POs, rubbish removers, and other service providers who may help someone with hoarding disorder during a project. It offers advice on how to support a client when interacting with other service providers, four alternative methods for decluttering, and an overview of the legal rights and responsibilities of a service provider in a hoarding situation. This training will help support any service worker who wishes to help someone with hoarding disorder.

Hoarding Home Solutions for Family and Friends

This course is for the family and friends of someone who struggles with hoarding disorder. A participant may have tried to help someone in the past but found it difficult and made little headway. This training offers twelve hours of education, workbooks, resource tools, and real-life stories to help cement the lessons. Helping someone with hoarding disorder can be demanding, and doubly so if the person is a close family member or friend. This course intends to educate and train the average person in techniques that can make an immediate difference in their loved one's life.

> https://hoardinghomesolutions.com.au/hoarding-home-solutions-courses

Clearing the Way Home

Susan Gardner is a Certified Professional Organizer in Chronic Disorganization (CPO-CD). She offers services to help clients organize their space and maintain a comfortable level of clutter.

Susan provides organizing help, hoarding disorder support, safe space creation, and training workshops. Her courses are dedicated to supporting individuals who want to make a life change that allows them to feel comfortable and content within their space.

https://www.clearingthewayhome.com/events

Time Space Organization (TSO)
The Zone Plan: A Method for Organizing Your Home

This teleclass is a ten-month program consisting of two thirty-minute private sessions each month. The course is intended to guide an individual through a full-home organization project, focusing on one area of a participant's home each month. The class also includes a PDF copy of Jonda Beattie's workbook, *From Vision to Victory*.

https://www.timespaceorg.com/teleclass

Organization Rules® Clutter Support Classes

Vickie Dellaquila, CPO, CPO-CD has been a professional organizer since 2002 and has created her business, Organization Rules®, Inc., to provide compassionate organizing for every stage of life. Vickie offers virtual organizing, chronic disorganization, hoarding services, and a Clutter

Support class. Her Clutter Support class is a six-week educational program that Vickie uses to help people learn how to recognize clutter, gather motivation, and effectively deal with the clutter in their space.

https://www.organizationrules.com/class

Clutter Support Class Topics of Discussion:

- Week 1: Clarification, insight, and project hierarchy
- Week 2: Goal setting, perfectionism, and accountability
- Week 3: Motivation and excuses
- Week 4: Personal clutter boundaries, plan for action
- Week 5: Non-acquiring exercise
- Week 6: The challenges of discarding

Vickie guides each participant as she creates a hierarchy of organizing projects. This list will serve as a guide for creating personal clutter boundaries and plans for action. Discarding and non-acquiring exercises followed by open discussion will help participants identify strengths and vulnerabilities. This class is for participants whose readiness for change is high. It's designed for people who have had issues with major clutter, can't seem to get control of it, keep backsliding, and don't know why. Vickie delves into reasons why people are holding onto objects and discusses emotional attachments that participants may have to their possessions.

Vickie shares who this class is best for. "People that have held on to things for a very long time and cannot identify for themselves what the reasons are. They have felt trapped by their clutter for so long but didn't know why. Members of the class avoid reviewing the items due to the emotions that they will have to experience by dealing with the stuff.

"Some people can do things on their own, and sometimes they do. But the classes allow collaboration with likeminded people, and can work with a therapist and possibly with a professional organizer on site."

Some students have signed up for the class because they have a significant other who can't live with the clutter anymore. Vickie keeps the groups small to build trust among members. "Most people find the support of the other attendees very helpful, and the privacy in this group is protected," Vickie promises.

Organization Rules, Inc. also offers a follow-up Clutter Maintenance class that lasts for three weeks. The maintenance course is designed to help keep people on track with their clutter goals and provide support to those who may have strayed from their plan.

METHOD 7

CLUTTER SUPPORT GROUPS

What can you expect when you join a support group? How is this different from a class? A support group is a collective gathering of minds, where stories and feelings are shared in order to provide ideas and find solutions. There's an agreement of anonymity among the participants, and the space created to communicate is intended to be judgment free. Support groups are intended to be a safe place to share feelings about how difficult it is to part with possessions, to organize surroundings, and to cope with frustrations of family members and friends who struggle with participants' living conditions.

Anonymity is sometimes an issue in virtual support groups. However, the same agreement made in in-person groups applies to virtual groups. To safeguard participants' privacy, a moderator or facilitator will never record a virtual support group. Further, participants who are uncomfortable being on camera can turn their camera off and still participate in the group. Participants who are comfortable can turn their camera on and share not only their face but also their space.

What is it like to actually be in a support group? Participation is essential. While members join a group to receive, they are also there to give. They could have creative solutions that might have a huge impact on someone in the group. Some groups allow crosstalk, and others don't. Crosstalk occurs when members of the group are allowed to discuss topics, feelings, and solutions without taking turns. Other groups will offer a hybrid option of letting everyone have a turn to speak, then open it up for discussion after everyone has had a chance to share.

Here are support groups that are easily accessible and continuously welcome new members:

Clutters Anonymous Meetings

Clutters Anonymous (CLA) offers free recurring meetings for its members. CLA schedules physical, virtual, and phone meetings every week. These meetings are intended to be a safe space for members to work together to utilize the twelve steps and twelve traditions to take control of their clutter situation. CLA offers different types of meetings, including traditional support groups, victories and goals sessions, organizing practice, and guided meditation/mindfulness. All CLA meetings offer assistance to anyone who's struggling with chronic disorganization.

https://clutterersanonymous.org

Steri-Clean Inc. Hoarders Support Groups

Steri-Clean, Inc. offers support to people who struggle with hoarding disorder by providing hoarding cleanup, item recovery, and an online hoarding support group. The support group meets every Sunday and Tuesday, using a web-based chat client. The group is completely anonymous, so anyone can feel comfortable talking about their struggles regarding hoarding disorder. Steri-Clean offers services and support to anyone who suffers from hoarding disorder or who has a loved one who's affected by it.

https://hoardingcleanup.com/hoarding_support_group

Release Repurpose Clutter Support Groups

Clear Space for You is an online clutter support group that meets once a week for four weeks for an hour and is run by Diane Quintana and Jonda Beattie. The group is limited to four participants to create a safe semiprivate space in which to share weekly wins and challenges. Diane and Jonda intentionally keep the group small so that each person receives plenty of individualized attention. In addition to individualized attention, each participant also receives a weekly journal where Diane and Jonda record the person's comments and a thirty-minute private phone consultation scheduled during the third or fourth session.

https://releaserepurpose.com/clear-the-clutter-support-group

METHOD 8

BOOKS AND RESEARCH PUBLICATIONS

Numerous publications are available to help someone get organized. Many books are available at your public library. They can also be purchased in print, digital, and audio formats.

ADD and ADHD

Change Your Habits: ADHD Style by Sue Fay West
ADD-Friendly Ways to Organize Your Life by Judith Kolberg and Kathleen Nadeau, Ph.D.
Delivered from Distraction: Getting the Most out of Life with Attention Deficit Disorder by Edward M. Hallowell and John R. Ratey

Chronic Disorganization and Hoarding Disorder

Conquering Chronic Disorganization by Judith Kolberg

ADD-Friendly Ways to Organize Your Life by Judith Kolberg and Kathleen Nadeau, Ph.D.

Stuff: Compulsive Hoarding and the Meaning of Things by Randy Frost and Gail Steketee

Digging Out: Helping Your Loved One Manage Clutter, Hoarding, and Compulsive Acquiring by Michael A. Tompkins and Tamara L. Hartl

Filled Up and Overflowing: What to do When Life Events, Chronic Disorganization, or Hoarding Go Overboard by Diane N. Quintana, CPO-CD, and Jonda Beattie, M.Ed.

Buried in Treasures: Help for Compulsive Acquiring, Saving, and Hoarding (Treatments That Work) by David Tolin and Randy O. Frost

From Hoarding to Hope: Understanding People Who Hoard and How to Help Them by Geralin Thomas

Making Peace with the Things in Your Life: Why Your Papers, Books, Clothes, and Other Possessions Keep Overwhelming You and What to Do About It by Cindy Glovinsky

Obsessive Compulsive Disorder

When Once Is Not Enough: Help for Obsessive-Compulsives by Gail Steketee and Kerrin White

Time Management

Time Management from the Inside Out by Julie Morganstern
Never Be Late Again by Donna DeLonzor
Time Management: How to Break the Late Habit, Embrace Punctuality, and Always Be On Time by Mike Hardy
Organizing Your Day: Time Management Techniques That Will Work for You by Sandra Felton and Marsha Sims
Perfecting the Lifestyle Called Punctuality: Become Time-Conscious Before it's Too Late by Jeremy Bolton

Shopping Addiction/Overspending

To Buy or Not to Buy: Why We Overshop and How to Stop by April Lane Benson, Ph.D.

Children's Disorganization

Benji's Messy Room by Diane N. Quintana, CPO-CD, and Jonda Beattie, M.Ed.
Suzie's Messy Room by Diane N. Quintana, CPO-CD, and Jonda Beattie, M.Ed.

Guides for Therapists

Behind the Closed Door: The Mental Stress of Physical Stuff by Katie Tracy

The Oxford Handbook of Hoarding and Acquiring edited by Randy O. Frost and Gail Steketee

Cognitive Therapy for Obsessive-Compulsive Disorder: A Guide for Professionals by Sabine Wilhelm, Ph.D., Gail Steketee, Ph.D., and Aaron T. Beck, MD (Foreword)

Overcoming Obsessive-Compulsive Disorder—Client Manual (Best Practices for Therapy) by Matthew McKay, Ph.D., and Gail Steketee, Ph.D.

METHOD 9

ONLINE RESOURCES

The following resources for locating assistance for chronic disorganization and hoarding behaviors can be accessed by visiting the websites below.

Professional Organizer Associations

Finding a PO who is right for you and your personal organizing journey is easier than ever with online directories in the following associations' websites:

Institute for Challenging Disorganization (ICD)

The Institute for Challenging Disorganization (ICD) is an association composed primarily of professional organizers, productivity specialists, and other service providers who recognize and wish to alleviate chronic disorganization in their clients. ICD provides education to facilitate a better understanding of what causes CD, such as hoarding disorder, and what techniques and strategies are most effective when working with a client. ICD offers classes to members and nonmembers once a week throughout the year.

https://www.challengingdisorganization.org

National Association of Productivity & Organizing Professionals (NAPO)

NAPO was founded by a small group of professional women in Los Angeles in the 1980s. The group became a destination for those who wanted to become POs and launch new careers. NAPO has since become nationally recognized as a leading organization for productivity and organizing professionals. The association has the authority to bestow the Certified Professional Organizer (CPO) credential to qualified members. NAPO offers yearly conferences and learning materials to drive continued education.

https://www.napo.net

National Association of Specialty and Senior Move Managers (NASMM)

NASMM is the leading association of Specialty and Senior Move Managers in the United States, Canada, and abroad. NASMM offers continued education opportunities to its members through its A+ accreditation and training program. NASMM members recognize the need for extra care and attentiveness when it comes to Senior Move Management and downsizing. Changing homes can be a difficult time, and seniors need additional support. NASMM provides a platform for professionals to educate themselves and provide the assistance the senior community needs.

https://www.nasmm.org

Japan Association of Life Organizers (JALO)

JALO, based in Japan, has been training organizing professionals since 2008. The organization provides and extensive list of courses to its members and trains them to be Life Organizers®. A Life Organizer is someone who helps a client organize their mind and lifestyle as well as their space. JALO members believe that an organized life will lead to an organized home.

https://jalo.jp

Nederlandse Beroepsvereniging van Professional Organizers (NBPO)

NBPO, based in The Netherlands, was founded in 1997. Its mission is to gather and share knowledge among its members. Members are offered regular training opportunities and occasions to work together. There's also a Members Only section of NBPO's website that contains additional educational materials. NBPO associates work together to enhance every member's skillset and further each professional's education.

https://nbpo.nl

Professional Organizers in Canada (POC)

POC gathers organizing professionals from various backgrounds and provides professional organizing training. POC organizes an annual conference and training programs to complement its members' educational objectives. POC members work together to enhance their organizing skills and offer better support to their clients.

https://www.organizersincanada.com

Association of Professional Declutters and Organisers (APDO)

APDO was founded in the United Kingdom in 2004. The association maintains an online directory to help clients find POs. It also offers training, mentoring, and networking to its members to facilitate educational and industry growth. APDO members gather together to educate themselves on professional organizing practices, because they understand their clients rely on their expertise.

https://www.apdo.co.uk

L'Associazione Professional Organizers Italia (APOI)

APOI provides educational and professional support for its members, including newsletters and blogs to increase interest in organizing. APOI assists clients in finding local POs and supports its members through educational resources and training opportunities.

https://www.apoi.it

Public Information Websites

The following websites offer information about various diagnoses and addictions that can coincide with or complicate hoarding disorder.

ADD/ADHD

ADDitude Magazine is a physical and digital magazine that focuses on the daily struggles someone with ADHD may face. The magazine offers support in recognizing ADHD, finding reputable doctors to diagnose ADHD, and provides insights into the lives of people with ADHD. The publication includes personal stories, vetted resources, and tips and tricks for living with ADHD or supporting a loved one with ADHD. The magazine's writers and its readers are dedicated to normalizing ADHD, while providing assistance to any who may need it.

https://www.additudemag.com/

Children and Adults with Attention-Deficit/ Hyperactivity Disorder

CHADD was founded in 1987 because living with ADHD can be an isolating experience. CHADD offers ADHD assistance through their information, support, and advocacy groups. CHADD has been petitioning lawmakers and school boards to create better ADHD compliance in home life and school life. CHADD welcomes new members and gives them a place to belong.

https://chadd.org

Chronic Disorganization (CD)

The Institute for Challenging Disorganization (ICD) is an association composed primarily of professional organizers, productivity specialists, and other service providers who recognize and wish to alleviate chronic disorganization in their clients. ICD provides education to facilitate a better understanding of what causes CD, such as hoarding disorder, and what techniques and strategies are most effective when working with a client. ICD offers classes to members and nonmembers once a week, throughout the year.

https://www.challengingdisorganization.org

Obsessive Compulsive Disorder

The International OCD Foundation (IOCDF) began in 1986 when a group of people affected by OCD came together to offer each other aid. This tradition has continued as IOCDF and has created a community of mutual support and understanding. The organization offers assistance to those seeking help for OCD. Members and site visitors are offered free

OCD education that breaks the stigma behind OCD. IOCDF intends to be a safe space for anyone affected by OCD and anyone who wants to support their loved one with OCD.

https://iocdf.org

Shopping and Debt Addictions

The Shulman Center offers a Shopaholics Anonymous support center. Available educational materials explain common sources of shopping addiction, discuss common trends in shopping addiction, and post warning signs of regression. The Shulman Center also provides access to therapy, consulting, and other support groups for people who experience shopping addiction. Shopaholics Anonymous provides a comprehensive resource list for anyone affected by shopping addiction and anyone looking to help a loved one.

https://theshulmancenter.com/overspending-shopping-addiction.html

Debtors Anonymous is a coalition of people dedicated to supporting others affected by shopping and debt addiction. Debtors Anonymous provides help finding support groups, educational materials, and professional help through their website. Due to the nature of debt, there may be countless legal forms someone has to sift through while trying to get a handle on their life. Debtors Anonymous will help connect debt professionals with people who require their assistance. Members of Debtors Anonymous understand that debt can be an addiction just like alcohol or drugs, and they're determined to support one another until they feel confident in themselves again.

https://debtorsanonymous.org

More internet resources can be found on our website at www.ImRightHereBook.com

METHOD 10

TELEVISION SHOWS

Professional organizing services gained popularity in the early 2000s with the appearance of television shows like *Clean Sweep* (TLC Network, 2003–2005) with Peter Walsh, and *Clean House* (Esquire Network, 2003) with Niecy Nash. The formula was simple. The client was greeted warmly by a professional organizer and the film crew. The PO and the audience watching at home toured the client's home to see how much stuff they had in the house, from piles of clothing not in closets to overcrowded common living spaces. The PO questioned the client, delving into the reasons for holding onto certain items.

Agreements were made between the PO and the client regarding what the goals were, and the sorting began. In the end, the client kept the items that meant the most to them and received a home makeover in the process. Millions of viewers from around the world tuned in each week to see a person's belongings piled up in their living, dining, and sleeping spaces. It was an incredible opportunity for those watching to learn about the various reasons—most of them sentimental but some based on perceived monetary value—we form attachment to things.

The emotions that we all saw in television bits were just the tip of the iceberg. The client, often coming from a place of shame and anxiety, was forced to reckon with the origin of their collecting and untidy behaviors. Most of the time, this was done with compassion and professionalism. These clients were interviewed and evaluated prior to the project being filmed and were chosen carefully. Those tuning in watched the client react as twenty people in matching T-shirts removed large amounts of possessions from their home and put their belongings outside on tarps, in donation trucks, and in dumpsters. They parted with many possessions in a short period of time, the PO coaching (and sometimes coaxing) them along the way. Some shows used a garage sale model at the end so the client could gain some return on their discarded items. This worked well for those who weren't experiencing hoarding tendencies. It even seemed like a viable solution for those with CD.

When *Hoarders* and *Hoarders: Buried Alive* were introduced into mainstream media, we were finally able to see how someone with a home full of accumulations could actually be helped using psychological intervention as well as compassionate professional assistance. The show revealed some homes that the viewing audience perceived as severe environments. I experienced such a situation when I was part of the organizing team on A&E's series, *Hoarders* (Season 11, "Sherry").

Sandy Kutchman, Ceri Binotto, and I went into the experience not knowing a lot about television production but having years of experience and education working with clients who have hoarding disorder. I'm a Certified Professional Organizer (CPO) and a member of NAPO, NASMM, and ICD. Sandy is a Certified Virtual Professional Organizer (CVPO) and a member of ICD and NAPO, and Ceri is a PO and Certified Senior Move Manager (SMM-C) and member of NASMM. The three of us showed up on the first day of filming to discover that the PO hired to be the lead organizer was unable to be present for the project. The home we were there to help organize had at least five feet of clutter. Doorways were virtually blocked with just three feet of space at the top for a person to crawl through.

The client, Sherry, confessed that she had built a wall of possessions to protect herself from the outside world. She worked with the show's psychologist, Dr. Tolin, who tried to help her understand how behavior changes could reduce the tremendous amount of accumulated items. She and the crew had four days of filming to move as much as possible. The situation was compounded by Sherry's son, Matt, who also lived in the home in his own hoarded space. Sherry and Matt's relationship off camera seemed amicable, but on camera, it was volatile, especially when Sherry's estranged daughter, Lauren, came to be a part of the process.

Cory Chalmers of Steri-Clean was in charge of the actual cleaning out of the home, while I was to create a system, behind the scenes, for sorting everything that the hauling crew, G.I.Haul, brought out of the house. Once they were sorted, Sherry could review the items and determine what to keep and what to let go.

The first thing to do was set up sorting stations. Each station would hold items of a specific category. We built more than fifty cardboard boxes that U-Haul, a sponsor, had provided. The hauling crew used these to carry out Sherry's things. We set up long folding tables and labeled them by category: clothing, shoes, coats, kitchen items, jewelry, personal care and first aid, blankets, electronics, and memorabilia. When the hauling crew brought out a box, we sorted the items as quickly as we could. Fortunately, at least that first day, we were able to dispatch all the items brought out to us onto the tables so we could discuss Sherry's decisions.

Sandy, Ceri, and I worked with Sherry to create the important rules around what we were allowed to discard and the number of items in each category she wanted to keep (for example, ten pairs of black pants, all coats, one of each kind of kitchen small appliance as long as it looked newer than the others, etc.). There were items that Sherry had an especially challenging experience with, and Dr. Tolin worked directly with her on camera to help her manage her emotions and decisions. Sherry had been amenable to the rules we set up with her, and we wanted to keep the momentum going. When she became frustrated, Dr. Tolin gently emphasized that she had a choice to have us there or not. Every day, she chose for us all to stay and help her.

On Day Three, we saw the hauling crew's morale shift when they had to go up to the second floor of the home. The upstairs bathroom was beyond repair, and the odor had an intense effect on the hauling team. Cory wasn't able to be present that day, so we stepped in to provide our direction.

Often, people who live with extremely hoarded homes don't recognize the smells and odors in their environment. Toilets are sometimes neglected in terms of cleaning, and bathtubs become places to store more belongings. The bathroom is often converted from a place for maintaining daily hygiene to a collection area. In some hoarded spaces, the toilets have to be replaced, or the entire bathroom has to be remodeled and pipes underneath have to be repaired. This was the case in this home, and professional plumbers were called in to do the work.

I set up a fireman's brigade to move the trashcans full of items the hauling crew brought down to our organizing team. I would take the trashcan from the hauling team member, Sherry would do her "once-over," and I would then give what remained to Ceri, who would take it to Sandy in the alley. Sandy would then give it to a hauler, who would empty it in the waiting dumpster. By late in the day, the level of items in the house had gone down but was still three feet deep. The crew was very frustrated at the pace at which items were leaving. The organizers, by now, knew which categories of items Sherry wanted to see and decide about, so it became easier for us to dispose of items not in those categories.

I asked the hauling crew to fill the bins with items that fit into "discard" categories and then pass them to each other until they reached the man at the window, who would dump them out into a waiting dumpster. Another crew member, in the dumpster, would rake the debris evenly in the dumpster. The empty cans were passed back and then returned full again. In this manner, we emptied most of Sherry's bedroom, all of Lauren's bedroom, part of Matt's room, and the second-floor landing. As we worked, we did our best to locate items Sherry and Lauren had been looking to save. All of us, the hauling crew and the organizing crew, kept our eyes peeled at all times for those things. We were able to find most of what Sherry was looking for, and when one of the hauling men found Lauren's pink prom dress from high school, I excitedly ran it down the stairs and presented it to her. She cried and thanked me profusely. There weren't many items that could be salvaged, but luckily that dress was in a closet that hadn't been accessed in a long time. The mountain of possessions outside the closet had barricaded the door.

Cory returned on Day Four to find that we had made a lot of progress. He decided it was time to start bringing in the outside technicians and cleaning team to make way for the final reveal. Sherry and Matt would receive all new kitchen appliances, a cleaned and sanitized kitchen and upstairs bathroom, a new hot water heater, HVAC, and electrical repairs. They received new furniture too—a table and chairs for the kitchen area and two full-sized beds with all of the linens. The beds were placed in Lauren's now empty bedroom.

Dr. Tolin offered Sherry aftercare services to support her after the project was complete. Aftercare services can include individual and family therapy, case management services from a mental health agency, and professional organizing services. Sherry seemed interested at first but ultimately refused the help, and eventually began hoarding her home again according to A&E. This type of relapse into older habits is called backsliding and is common when continued support is either not provided or not available. It takes tremendous effort to commit to creating and sustaining new habits, and with CD and hoarding behaviors, the road seems to be more challenging.

When we work with a client who's exhibiting hoarding behaviors, they'll mention that the method used on the TV show is not a realistic solution for them. We explain that more than the four days given on the show is necessary to make decisions in a healthy and professional, guided and paced manner. However, clients on the show have agreed to the show's method in order to get the help that they need at the time.

It's important to note that there are always lessons to be learned by watching shows that help those who are hoarding. If the dramatic moments can be put aside, the teaching moments will appear, especially during the segments where the psychologist or psychiatrist discusses behavior change strategies with the client, as well the reasons why aftercare would create a sustaining and positive support system.

Janine Adams shared her thoughts on her own TV appearance. "I did work on a *Hoarding: Buried Alive* episode with fifty-five-year-old twins, who had in five years hoarded the house so that it could not be entered. I stayed out in the yard with the clients, and the junk guys brought the items out for us to review. It was a home that truly was a filled with hazardous waste. They wanted to keep everything, but could only keep [items made of] plastic because it was the only thing that could be sanitized." Before Janine and the clients could look at anything to decide upon its value, it had to be sanitized. During the episode's filming, the house unfortunately was condemned due to an unstable floor.

Janine provided aftercare services for the clients. Because they couldn't go back to their home, Janine worked with them elsewhere. "I went to work with them on life skills in a nearby small hotel room once per week, but their room kept filling up with food. I tried to take them on a 'non-shopping' trip at Wal-Mart, but one of the twins flew off the handle, having a public tantrum, after being reminded that that item wasn't on the list, which I believe were hamburger buns."

Jonda Beattie has appeared on *Hoarding: Buried Alive* along with Judith Kolberg (Season 1, Episode 2, "Beyond Embarrassment") and on *Hoarders* with Diane Quintana (Season 4 Episode 1, "Phyllis/Janet"). She shared some of her experiences, summarizing how frustrating it was for her to not have more follow-through after the show concluded. "The end was not enough for me. The client needed more counseling. The client really needs to be committed and have a strong motivation for change, which is NOT fast. If we get twenty-five percent of the client's goal met on those shows, we feel really good, that we have done 'change,' maintaining a lifestyle for them. We are making their homes livable. They are going to different groups for support and seem to be living a better quality of life."

Vickie Dellaquila also appeared on a *Hoarding: Buried Alive* episode (Season 7, Episode 8, "Lynn/Kyle"). She and her organizing team showed compassion to the woman they helped and worked side by side with a local hauler, Junk King, as well as a therapist and a cleaning team. Vickie encouraged Lynn (the client) during the entire process, saying things like "Good, you let a lot go; you should really be proud of yourself."

After the project was complete, Vickie was optimistic, stating that to move forward, Lynn needed to continue with therapy and continue with a professional organizer. Vickie feels that the TV shows are truly about bringing the awareness of the issue to the public. "The shows also support this population by telling them that they are not alone, and that there is help," she says.

Diane Quintana worked as a PO on A&E's *Hoarders* (Season 4 Episode 1, "Phyllis/Janet"). The show paid Diane's fees over six months after the show ended to continue to work with that family. Diane shared her hopeful insight into the plight and possible solution that could truly assist those with hoarding disorder. "In every neighborhood in every city there is ONE home that needs this type of support and assistance. I don't care where you are in the USA, you can find at least ONE home. The focus, if anything, needs to be on safety. Fire and police departments need to be interested in this." Diane explained the ideal way these families could be supported by their communities. "In a perfect world, there would be funds available, where organizations would write in to groups for grants, money set aside by a municipality, township, etcetera, to help those families that are challenged in such a way. When you get the church organizations and such together, a small portion of that grant could help fix a leaky roof and make a safer home, encompassing many different ways to make that happen. It has to come from the town, though. There has to be an application and approval process, much like the way people apply to be on TV for charitable works."

"I think every single person alive has mental health issues," Sheila Delson says. However, she wants the world to understand this very special population. When it comes to CD and her clients who hoard, she says that while they suffer from mental illness, they're not incapable of thinking. She describes the people she has helped as beloved clients (even the very challenging ones) and says the majority of them are warm, right-brained, creative, very much in-tune to others, and hypertensive to the world around them. They're often misinterpreted individuals, especially when we watch shows like *Hoarding: Buried Alive* and *Hoarders*. These shows are designed to inspire and educate the public and to help families help their loved ones who have hoarding behaviors. It's important to not overlook the importance of understanding the mental health aspects that are addressed on the programs.

"On TV, we see people taking the emotionally charged item and chucking it into the garbage can, and this is what the population sees as the norm. This perspective is what we have to change." She approaches her clients who have CD and those who have hoarding behaviors differently, due to the vast spectrum of mental health issues with each client. "It's about *them* emotionally, and how they connect with their stuff."

AFTERWORD

After reading this book and reviewing the resources within, I am hoping that you have learned that there are many safe and beneficial ways to get help for hoarding and chronic disorganization. Possibly, the assistance you are seeking is for a family member, a partner, a neighbor, or a friend. You could also be an allied mental health professional who is seeking ways to talk to your client who is challenged daily by their home environment and making difficult decisions about their belongings. Not all of the information in this book will apply to everyone in need of support and guidance, but I am hopeful that at least one option looks attainable. I want to reiterate that many of the methods can be in use at one time, such as attending a support group while working with a virtual organizer coach.

I am also optimistic that someday there will be a hoarding task force in every community, county, and in every city in the world that would be in place to address the issues that are presented to individuals who are struggling with a crippling sense of disorganization and homes that feel burdensome, inescapable, and unmanageable.

If any of the methods described in this book interest you, I invite you to explore them, knowing that we are right here, waiting to help you. If you or someone you care about is still hesitant about calling a professional organizer, this is normal and understandable. Here are some final words of inspiration and support from one of the POs featured in this book:

"When I can tell that it's been difficult for a person to reach out for help, I'll say to them, 'Congratulations on taking this first step to ask for help. Sometimes that's the hardest part of the whole process.' That usually leads to a discussion of how other clients have experienced similar trepidation and how we've been able to help them. When I can normalize the fear, it usually makes them more comfortable and allows a conversation to open up so that I can answer questions and perhaps relieve some of the fear. I think it's really important to acknowledge, but not minimize, the fear." Janine Adams

APPENDIX

The Clutter Quality of Life Scale

The Clutter Quality of Life Scale (CQLS) has been designed by the Institute for Challenging Disorganization (ICD) to help people assess for themselves the personally felt impact that clutter has on their well-being. The scale includes eighteen statements. Please read each statement carefully and circle the response that best represents your feelings. Keep in mind there are no "right" or "wrong" answers. Your honest response to each statement is what matters. The scale can be found on the ICD® website (www.challengingdisorganization.org).

The ICD Clutter–Hoarding Scale

The Clutter–Hoarding Scale is an assessment measurement tool developed by the Institute for Challenging Disorganization (ICD) to give professional organizers and related professionals definitive parameters related to health and safety. ICD is a

I'm Right Here

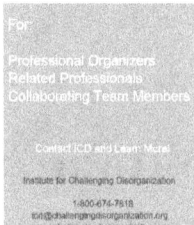

nonprofit 501(c)(3) educational organization whose mission is to benefit people challenged by chronic disorganization.

The Clutter-Hoarding Scale (C-HS) can be found, along with other resources, on the ICD website.

www.challengingdisorganization.org

ICD Certification Overview

ICD Certificate and Specialist Levels

ICD provides five levels of certificates and certification, all focused on chronic disorganization, a holistic approach to working with organizing and productivity clients. With five levels, as you grow your business, your education continues to meet your needs.

Chronic Disorganization is not a medical diagnosis, but the word "chronic" does acknowledge a lifelong struggle. The subscribers of ICD look at many situations and conditions that affect CD. ICD education is focused on educating our subscribers to assist their clients affected by chronic disorganization.

Foundation Certificate (Basic CD)

- Required for being included in the ICD referral directory.
- Prerequisite for Level II Chronic Disorganization Specialist Certificate.
- Required to advance to any of the Level II Specialist Certificates.

Level I Certificates of Study

- Basic plus specialized education on issues, concepts, and challenges presented by client work.
- Classes are given by mental health and wellness professionals (social workers, licensed professional counselors, psychologists, etc.), and various organizing and productivity professionals inside and outside the field.
- ICD subscribers who hold a Level I Certificate of Study have completed six hours of education specific to that subject area.

ADHD – Certificate of Study in ADHD

ADM – Certificate of Study in Client Management (formerly Client Administration)

AGE – Certificate of Study in Understanding the Needs of the Aging Client

HIC – Certificate of Study in Health Issues and Conditions and the Client Affected by CD

HRD – Certificate of Study in Hoarding Issues

INT – Certificate of Study in Interpersonal Intelligence

LT – Certificate of Study in Life Transitions and the Client Affected by CD

SLT – Certificate of Study in Student and Learning Theories

TMP – Certificate of Study in Time Management and Productivity

Level II Specialist Certificates

- Broader and deeper specialized topic education on issues, concepts, and challenges presented by client work.
- ICD subscribers who hold a Level II CD Specialist have completed approximately twenty-five hours of education on Chronic Disorganization.
- Subscribers who hold the ADHD, Aging, or Hoarding Specialist Certificate have completed an additional twenty-five hours of education specific to the specialist subject area.

CD Specialist
ADHD Specialist
Hoarding Specialist
Aging Specialist

Level III Certified Professional Organizer in Chronic Disorganization

- This is ICD's Certification Level, and the first of two leading industry certifications.
- Each candidate is assigned an experienced CPO-CD program mentor and works one-on-one, in completion of a seventeen to twenty month program.
- A CPO-CD is a professional organizer who has been educated in depth on the issues of chronic disorganization.

- The CPO-CD program uses various educational formats so the student can apply the education, during the program, with current clients and work with the program mentor on results and challenges.

Level IV Communication Mentor

- Develop skills and knowledge in the areas of training, presenting, coaching, motivation, communication, and leadership.
- Practical applications include volunteering as an Education Mentor working with subscribers on their educational needs and goals.
- This level also prepares one for Level V, which includes being a Program Mentor to a CPO-CD student candidate.

Level V Master Trainer in CD and Organization Overview

- Develop and/or deepen leadership, publication, and training skills; provide service, and commitment to the field of study and exploration of Chronic Disorganization and Organization/Productivity.
- This is the ICD certificate and certification program's highest level of achievement.
- Part of this role is to mentor a CPO-CD student candidate.

The Professionals in this Book

Linda Samuels, CPO-CD®, CVPO™ is the Past President of ICD®. She was ICD®'s first Marketing Director, is an ICD® Program Mentor and Master Trainer, and is a NAPO Golden Circle member. Linda is the author of *The Other Side of Organized, Finding Balance Between Chaos and Perfection*.

Janine Adams, CPO®, has been a Certified Professional Organizer since 2005 and owns Peace of Mind Organizing. She has written more than a dozen digital guidebooks, served on the board of ICD®, served three separate terms as President of the St. Louis Chapter of NAPO, and appeared on TV shows like A&E's *Hoarders* and TLC's *Hoarding: Buried Alive*, as well as morning talk shows like *Great Day St. Louis*.

Sue West, CPO-CD®, MA, Clinical Mental Health Counseling, ICD® Master Trainer, is a past president of ICD®, and before becoming a therapist, she was a Certified Organizer Coach specializing in ADHD. She is the author of *Change Your Habits, ADHD Style* and *Organize for a Fresh Start: Embrace Your Next Chapter in Life*.

Alice Price, CPO-CD®, COC, is an organizer, coach, author, speaker, and president of Organize Long Island, Inc., which she founded in 2002. She is a proud member of NAPO. Alice earned her specialist certificate in Hoarding and ADD as well as Chronic Disorganization. Alice contributed two sections to the book *The ICD® Guide to Challenging Disorganization for Professional Organizers*. Alice is a Certified Organizer Coach, credentialed by the Institute for Applied Coaching™.

Cris Sgrott, CPO®, CPO-CD®, SMM-C, ICD® Master Trainer founded Organizing Maniacs®, LLC, in 2007. She's a productivity consultant, organizer coach, and professional speaker. She's an active member of NAPO and also of CHADD, where she's co-chairing the annual conference for the third time. She has also co-contributed articles to CHADD's *Attention* magazine.

Denise Lee, CPO®, CSA, founded Clear Spaces in 2006. She's an organizer coach who has achieved multiple certifications from ICD®, including Chronic Disorganization (CD) Specialist. ADD Specialist. and Hoarding Specialist. She's received Level 1 Certifications in Understanding the Needs of the Student CD Client, Life Transitions, and Understanding the Needs of the Elderly CD Client.

Sheila Delson, CPO-CD®, is a cofounder of ICD® and cocreator of the respected ICD® Clutter-Hoarding Scale. She served on the ICD® board of directors in the roles of president, past president, and certification director. Sheila founded Free Domain Concepts, LLC in 1994. She has received the NAPO Founder's Award, the Service to NAPO Award, and the Judith Kolberg Highlighter Award through ICD®. She has been the keynote speaker at two Japan Association of Life Organizers (JALO) Conferences and was the first in the world to offer training and certification in Virtual Professional Organizing.

Vickie Dellaquila, CPO®, CPO-CD®, ICD® Master Trainer, is a member of ICD® and NAPO. She founded Organization Rules®, Inc. in 2002. Her books include *Don't Toss My*

Memories in the Trash: A Step-by-Step Guide to Helping Seniors Downsize, Organize, and Move and *The Moving Workbook*. Vickie has also contributed to *The ICD® Guide to Challenging Disorganization for Professional Organizers*.

Diane Quintana, CPO®, CPO-CD®, ICD® Master Trainer, is a member ICD® and NAPO and owner of DNQ Solutions. She's certified in chronic disorganization through ICD® and holds a degree as Hoarding and Attention Deficit Disorder specialist. She's an accomplished author of four organizing books, two of which she co-authored with Jonda Beattie, with whom she co-owns Release, Repurpose, Reorganize.

Jonda Beattie, M.Ed., is a Professional Organizer, owner of Time Space Organization, and co-owner of Release, Repurpose, Reorganize. She is a long-time member of ICD® and NAPO; she is a talented speaker and author, having co-authored three books on organizing with Diane Quintana, with whom she also runs a clutter support group. She writes regular blog posts on her website and offers virtual organizing services.

ACKNOWLEDGMENTS

This book was an entirely different book until my fiancé, Paul Diana, gave it a long and scrupulous read. It was his suggestion to make this a resource guide instead of the original direction it was headed. I am extremely grateful to him for not only taking the time to pour over the manuscript, but to be brave enough to tell me to scrap it and start over.

A special thanks to my daughter Mary Yesko, who made Chapter 10 more readable and who gave me her honest feedback, as always, as my editor-in-chief of not only my wardrobe, but my words. I can always count on her to tell me the truth, and I am a better writer and mother for it.

My son and company CIO, Nathan Yesko, and the entire team at Discover Organizing Inc. provided an ongoing and steady stream of support while I devoted more time to writing and speaking, and less time to incoming clients. Ceri Binotto and Sandy Kutchman not only handled the larger workload with professionalism and grace but were also my team members on the Hoarders show. They, and all of our employees truly know how to make my job easier by being so consistently caring every day. Our company is nothing without our team.

Sharon Fanning has been my friend since we were very young, running around in Norristown, Pa., and being my unpaid therapist, coach, and proofreader. If I had a fan club, Sharon would not only run it, but would probably recruit unwilling members off the street if she could, on a daily basis. If everyone had a Sharon, they would be the luckiest person alive.

Vickie Dellaquila, my colleague and dear friend, was sitting next to me at the ICD Conference when this idea was born, and excitedly and immediately began listing the names of the organizers in this book for me to interview. I appreciate her believing in this idea of mine in particular, and all of them, frankly.

My passion for mental health began during my first job in case management, at Central MH/MR of Montgomery County in Norristown, Pa., in 1990. Dave Wilkinson gave me my first chance to shine in the field, fresh out of Villanova University, and helped me to find an incredible circle of friends to work alongside of. Missy, Marco, Marni, Toni, Lorraine, Megan and Kelly, I especially thank you and so many others for showing up for your clients and patients and impacting so many lives to this day. You are my original and enduring tribe, and I love you all.

Finally, I want to thank Jenn T. Grace, of Publish Your Purpose Press, who helped me bring this very important project to the finish line. I could not have pulled this off without her, and she and her team of editors and artists are incredibly talented and generous.

ABOUT THE AUTHOR

Jill Yesko, CPO®, CPPO, who has a background in social work and human resources, founded Discover Organizing Inc.® in 2003. She formed her company on the principles of compassion and education—helping those in need learn how to create lasting systems of organization. Through her many years in business, Jill added move management services for families and seniors, and an on-demand bin storage company, which she has franchised. Jill appeared in Season 11 of *Hoarders* where she and her team help to clear a heavily hoarded home in Wheeling, West Virginia.

Jill became a member of the National Association of Productivity & Organizing Professionals in (NAPO) in 2004, earning a Certified Professional Organizer® designation in 2007. To fill her customer's growing needs, Jill expanded her service menu and started providing photo organizing, then life transition services, such as packing and unpacking services, which led to her becoming a member of the National Association of Senior Move Managers (NASMM).

She has trained her team of compassionate, detail-oriented professional organizers and senior move managers to exhibit her high level of professionalism and client care, and constantly endeavors to have Discover Organizing continue to be the most trusted organizing firm in the Greater Pittsburgh area.

Jill has two adult children, Nathan who is involved in the organizing business, and Mary who is a geoscientist. She lives in Pittsburgh with her fiancé and their two dogs and loves to surf, swim, and snowboard whenever she can.

HIRE JILL TO SPEAK

Inspire and educate your audience with Jill Yesko, Certified Professional Organizer®, author and professional speaker at your next event. Jill is a diverse and talented presenter with experience as an accomplished keynote speaker, masterclass thought leader, meeting facilitator, workshop leader or trainer.

Jill Yesko is a Certified Virtual Speaker through the National Speakers Association. She has been the keynoter and breakout presenter at many national conferences, both in person and virtual, for over ten years. Jill engages her audience with storytelling, interaction and powerful imagery, all while sharing her humor and revealing true stories of resiliency, bravery and empowerment. Every speaking presentation offers curated and customized content for each audience, and national associations have asked her to come back year after year to deliver new and captivating content.

Her topics include the "The Power of Productivity", "Engaging the Aging: Compassionate Ways to Care for Older Adults", and "Get Organized for Good". Her business-focused presentations help entrepreneurs to build stronger businesses, at whatever stage they are in their growth.

"It's not easy to motivate others to change lifelong habits. Jill Yesko is one of those professionals who exudes both the expertise and the heart that engenders respect and inspires change. She combines decades of practical experience and a deep personal understanding of people in a way that is both interesting and compelling. Not only do you pay attention, you are drawn into her passion to try something better. Jill has a commitment to her topic that translates easily to her audience. This is clearly someone who practices what she preaches, who has explored every excuse, challenge, and obstacle; and has found practical and positive solutions that really help. With a human, approachable style, Jill engages the real world issues of her audience, offers smalls steps to big success, and outlines realistic and helpful plans, tools, and tips. Each time we have hosted one of her presentations, she has been well received and has helped us to grow our business. She has my highest recommendation."

Bill Hull, Senior Living Sales Director,
Senior Presbyterian Care—Longwood at Oakmont.

To hire Jill to speak, visit her speaker's website at www.JillYesko.com

ABOUT DISCOVER ORGANIZING

Discover Organizing Inc. was founded in 2003 by Jill Yesko as a home organizing service. The company quickly expanded its service menu to include photo organizing, productivity and small business consulting, and senior move management services. The company was built on the principal that anyone who reaches out for help will receive it, and through their comprehensive community resource lists, they match every client with the right help for them—even if it is another organizing company.

Their mission is to listen to the client's concerns, identify their needs, and respond with expert services in a supportive, cheerful, and non-judgmental way. Discover Organizing values kindness, empathy, and compassion toward all clients and toward each other.